Last
of the
King's Heirs

Last
of the
King's Heirs

The **Untold Story**

Xulon Press

Xulon Press
555 Winderley Pl, Suite 225
Maitland, FL 32751
407.339.4217
www.xulonpress.com

© 2024 by Danny L Jones

All rights reserved solely by the author. The author guarantees all contents are original and do not infringe upon the legal rights of any other person or work. No part of this book may be reproduced in any form without the permission of the author.

Due to the changing nature of the Internet, if there are any web addresses, links, or URLs included in this manuscript, these may have been altered and may no longer be accessible. The views and opinions shared in this book belong solely to the author and do not necessarily reflect those of the publisher. The publisher therefore disclaims responsibility for the views or opinions expressed within the work.

Unless otherwise indicated, Scripture quotations taken from the Holy Bible, New International Version (NIV). Copyright © 1973, 1978, 1984, 2011 by Biblica, Inc.™. Used by permission. All rights reserved.

Paperback ISBN-13: 978-1-66289-640-8
Ebook ISBN-13: 978-1-66289-641-5

CONTENTS

Introduction vii

Chapter 1 - The Forgotten Kings 1

Chapter 2 - The Generations of Roswell King 17
    I. These are the Generations of
        Thomas "Captain Timothy" King. 17
    II. These are the generations of Roswell King Sr.. 18
    III. Slavery in Liberty County 21
    IV. Christianity and Slaves' Genealogy 26
    V. Unjust Men toward Their Slaves. 29
    VI. These are the generations of Roswell King III 33

Chapter 3 - Roswell King III's Second Family's Lineage 37
    I. These are the untold stories of
        Roswell King III and Mariah Guerard's Children 40
    II. These are Roswell King III and
        Mariah Guerard's grandchildren 52
    III. The content of the two-page letter
        from Frederick reads. 58
    IV. The King's life after the move from South Hampton Island . . . 60

Chapter 4 - The Land at Roswell King's
        South Hampton Plantation 65
    I. Skeletal remains

Chapter 5 - The Inheritance 77
    I. Seems to be a pattern. vii
    II. Looking for the second family. vii

A Prayer for the King Family 89
The Genealogy of Roswell King III's Second Family. 93
Sources. 95
Photograph Credits 97

Introduction:

It is a fact that most people want to know about their family history. We all are curious about the past because the past can tell us many things that we do not know about ourselves or our family history. It is human nature to want to know where we came from and who our ancestors and other relatives were. We also want to know our kinship ties to them, how they lived, the events that occurred in their daily lives, and what effect they have on our lives today.

To find out more about our family history, we can search and retrieve information from many different sources. We can search the internet or read books that may have been written about our family. We can search for documents such as court records, newspaper articles, personal letters, diaries, census, or vital records such as birth and death records. We can even receive family history through word of mouth and oral storytelling that was told from generation to generation by our ancestors. Storytellers can share information that cannot be found in history books or documents.

Knowing about one's family can be of significant importance in a person's life, such as mine or yours. What if you had an important person in your family? What if they were kings and queens, or of some other royalty status? What if they were slaves or slave owners? What if they were powerful and wealthy people and you are due to become an heir and inherit things from a deceased relative?

This book is filled with history, drama, betrayal, and conspiracy. It begins with life stories told by my grandmother, Annie (King) Wilkins. She told stories of her life growing up on South Hampton Island. South Hampton Island is mentioned many times in this book and can be identified by three different names: South Hampton Plantation, South Hampton Island, and South Hampton Preserve. She also gives a brief generational lineage of the King family and how she is related to the surnames of Roswell King.

This is the real life of Roswell King III's second family, their stories, and how they are related to this powerful and wealthy man, Roswell King Sr. The chapters in this book will give you stories and a brief background documentary of Roswell King's family. The stories were told by my ancestors. The other storylines are actual events that have been documented in books and court records. This documentary captured in this book will also help to identify the characters in the book, and to what extent they have on the Black King family life today.

Two King men were some of the south's most cruel slave masters. One is Roswell King Sr., the founder of the city of Roswell, Georgia. This book tells about the life he lived during the early and mid-1800s, and how he treated enslaved families on the plantation. And the second King man is Roswell King Jr., the son of Roswell King Sr. He too was a cruel slave master and the right hand of his father.

Roswell King III was the third generation; he was the son of Roswell King Jr. and the grandson of Roswell King Sr. He was not a cruel slave master like his father and grandfather. He was more accepted by others. Roswell III was known to have had two families—one white family and a Black family.

He became estranged from his first family and built a life with his second family against the approval of the other King relatives. Betrayal and turmoil came onto the second family after the death of Roswell III. And there was a hidden secret that was deliberately kept away from the rightful owner—by their hereditary right—of the King family's inheritances.

The second family of Roswell III is the forgotten King family. And they are the last of Roswell King's heirs who never received their inheritance. Peter C. Newman once said, "The rich don't have children; they have heirs."

The pictures in this book are from some of Eva (King, later Cook) Jones' personal collection of photographs and paintings. Eva is the daughter of Roswell King III from his second family. She gave her collection of

Introduction:

photographs and paintings to her grandnephew to have before her death. His family authorized the use of the pictures in this book. And the other pictures are from Frances "Babe" (King, later Caple) Curtis' photo album. Frances is the granddaughter of Roswell King III from his second family. She gave her pictures to her niece to have before her death. Her family authorized the use of the pictures in this book.

Chapter 1

The Forgotten Kings

My grandmother was a great storyteller. While I was growing up in southeastern Georgia, as a child she told some fascinating stories about her childhood and the place where she grew up. My grandmother Annie (King) Wilkins is better known by her childhood nickname, Sissy. The name Sissy was given to her by her siblings and was short for *sister*. Sissy was humble, kindhearted, and courageous, and she was a religious woman. She was born on South Hampton Island on September 23, 1911, just six days after the death of her grandfather, Roswell King III. Sissy had many childhood memories from growing up in South Hampton Island. This tract of land was once a slave plantation that was called South Hampton Plantation. It was owned by her grandfather Roswell King Jr., a slave owner. He was a member of the King family in coastal Georgia.

During the summer months in the 1970s and 1980s, while schools were out, we spent our summer days at our grandparents' house. Their house was like a second home for all of the grandchildren. When our parents went to work, the grandchildren would gather at our grandparents' house to play on her front porch, and under the big old oak tree in their front yard. It was the perfect place to cool off and avoid the roasting Georgia sun. We lived in a very close-knit neighborhood in Riceboro, Georgia, on the same country dirt road, which was called the Bay. The Bay was short for Briar Bay Road, which was our town's community road.

Our grandfather Josh Wilkins, Sissy's husband, would take Sissy grocery shopping once a week at Frank Hodges's Groceries off Highway US

17 in Riceboro. She would bring back all sorts of goodies and treats for the grandchildren, such as candies, cookies, and fruits, along with any of our requests.

Some of our favorite treats she made for us during those raging summer days were homemade ice cream and blackberry doobie, also known as blackberry cobbler. While Sissy was in the kitchen making the blackberry doobie, the grandchildren would be on the front porch churning the homemade ice cream. We would take turns churning the hand-cranked ice cream maker that held up under the pressure of our anxious and zealous hands.

With ice cream and blackberry doobie in our bowls, we all would gather around Sissy on her front porch while she sat in her rocking chair. She would rock back and forth in her chair and begin to tell us stories. She vividly etched mental pictures in our minds and on our hearts about the Bible, the King's family history, as well as her life as a child growing up on South Hampton Island. South Hampton Island is located in the coastal region of Georgia between Savannah and Jekyll Island.

We were mesmerized by every word she uttered from her mouth. One of the stories Sissy told us was about a haint, which is an old southern word for a type of ghost or spirit. The name *haint* is a Gullah Geechee word that is believed to derive from the word *haunt*. The Gullah people are African-American slaves who lived in the Low Country regions of coastal Georgia, coastal South Carolina, and northeastern coastal Florida.

Sissy would say, "We used to see ghosts when we used to live on South Hampton Island. Haints were bad back in those days." The haints she was referring to were spirits, restless or lost souls. Sissy continued by saying, "Haints used to ride us in our sleep all night long. When I lay down to sleep, I would sleep on my back. Just as I began to fall asleep, I could feel a presence in my room. Then I would hear noises, footsteps, voices, knocking, and thumping on the floors and walls. Then my body would become motionless. I was fully conscious as I tried to move to get out of bed, but I couldn't move any parts of my body. It was like I was paralyzed. I wasn't dreaming. I would try to speak or yell so I could get my mama's attention, but I could not even make a sound. Suddenly, I could feel something sitting on my chest, and I could barely breathe because the haint was on top of me, riding me. I was so scared! I started to scream. And again no sound came out of my mouth. The weight on my chest was getting heavier and heavier, making it harder to breathe. I thought I was going to suffocate. Then a small voice came into my head and said, 'Pray.' So I started praying; I started to pray the 'Our Father' prayer.: 'Our Father who art in heaven, Hallowed be thy name, thy Kingdom come, Thy will be done on earth as it is in heaven.' As I continued with the prayer, I could feel the haint getting off my chest and releasing me. Yeah, chillen, haint was bad back in those days." *Chillen* is an old southern word that means "children" or "many kids."

Today the phenomenon she described is known as sleep paralysis. Different cultures have many different names for what she described. In the deep southern states, it is called haint or sometimes old hag. There were paranormal phenomena on South Hampton Island and in the house of the King family. As a little girl, Sissy recalled seeing spirits or ghosts in the form or shape of human-like bodies appearing out of nowhere, floating or gliding across the room, and through walls. The spirits or ghosts were like lost, wandering souls trapped between this world and the next. Other family members in the household experienced the same phenomenon.

The King family believed the ghosts or haints were spirits of the dead buried in the graves of long-deceased family members in the graveyard not too far from their house on South Hampton Island. They also believed that the ghosts or haints were restless spirits haunted by the death of slaves from the past who chose death over slavery.

These spirits were believed to have been rebelled slaves from the ship of the transatlantic shipment of slaves in 1803. This was one of the largest mass suicides of enslaved Africans in history and occurred off the coast of Georgia. Many captured Africans on board the slave ship committed suicide by jumping off and drowning. Others believed when the ship docked, they just walked over into the water and drowned. These Africans just wanted to be free from captivity. Many of the slave bodies were washed up on the shores of coastal Georgia near Saint Simons Island.

Another ghost story Sissy told us pertained to when she was about thirteen years old. The incident happened on one warm summer evening. The King family went to visit other family members elsewhere. They were traveling on a mule and wagon down a dirt road surrounded by wooded areas. The family was leaving the Chapman community in Riceboro to go back home to South Hampton Island. On the wagon were Sissy; her father, Hardee King; her mother, Rosa (Quarterman) King; and two of her siblings.

Sissy said in a grim tone of voice, "Me, my daddy, my mama, and my sisters were traveling down a dirt road one evening on a mule and wagon coming from my grandmama's house in Chapman. It was dust-dark on the way back home. We looked ahead of us, and there stood a big tall man standing in the middle of the road with his arms spread wide apart. He was so tall. He looked to be over nine feet tall in the eyes of a five-foot-tall little girl. He looked to be as tall as Goliath. The same Goliath that fought David in the book of 1 Samuel. The tall man stood there with his arms spread outward blocking our path on the road. The mule got frightened and stopped, and then started moving back like it was panicking. My daddy had to get the mule under control. Once he settled the mule down, he looked back up and saw the man in the road."

Sissy's father, Hardee, called out to the man and said, "Move out the way! We're trying to get past." But the tall man just stood there with his arms still spread wide apart. Hardee shouted out again, "Where you come from!" The tall entity of a man looked at them in the wagon and said nothing. As he stood there with his arms spread wide, the tall figure of a man blew white smoke out of his mouth. Then the tall man said in a loud, deep, thundering voice, "Go back! I will not let you pass!" The tall man on the road kept repeating, "Go back! I will not let you pass!" So Sissy's father decided to turn the mule and wagon around and go the other way, back to Chapman.

Sissy stated, "After my daddy turned the mule and wagon around, we looked back toward the tall man, and he was gone. It was like he had disappeared out of thin air. So we traveled back to Chapman. The next morning, we found out that there was a fire on that same dirt road that engulfed the whole road and wooded area. If we had continued down that dirt road, that fire would've trapped us and burned us up."

As of this day, we don't know if the big tall man who stood blocking their path on the dirt road was an actual man, an angel, a spirit from the nearby graveyard, or a ghost of a lost soul from the early 1800s who died and washed up on the shores of coastal Georgia.

Sissy was a spiritual woman who went to church every Sunday morning, as did everyone in the household. She talked to us about the Bible every chance she got. And she loved to sing church hymns. Sissy was not a member of the church choir, but she always sat in the front row of the church and played along with her tambourine as the choir would sing. One of her favorite songs she sang for us was an old Negro spiritual hymn called "Walk with Me Lord." Sissy said the hymn encourages us to trust in the Lord Jesus. Even though the journey of life can be long, tiresome, and frustrating at times, Jesus will always be with you if you asked him to.

Sitting in the rocking chair on her front porch, she would rock slowly, patting her feet, and with her head held low, she would sing her favorite song with emotion and passion:

> Walk with me Lord, please walk with me.
> Walk with me Lord, walk with me.
> While I'm on this tedious journey.
> I want Jesus, walk with me.
> Hold my hand Lord, please hold my hand.
> Hold my hand Lord, hold my hand.
> While I'm on this tedious journey.
> I want Jesus, hold my hand.
> Be my friend Lord, please be my friend.
> Be my friend Lord, be my friend.
> While I'm on this tedious journey.
> I need Jesus, to be my friend.
> Don't leave me alone Lord, don't leave me alone.
> Don't leave me alone Lord, don't leave me alone.
> While I'm on this tedious journey.
> I need you Jesus, don't leave me alone.

One of the biblical stories Sissy told us was a story that was told to her as a little girl by her grandmother Mariah Guerard while living on South Hampton Island. The story was about Abraham. As a young man, Abraham worked in his father's idol shop. Abraham believed in one God. Sissy would say, "As a young man, Abraham was trying to convince his father, Terah, that there is one God that is the creator of everything. In those days, most people worshipped idols. One day, Abraham's father left him alone to mind the store. While his father was gone, Abraham took a hammer and destroyed all of the idols in the store except for the largest idol. Abraham put the hammer in the hand of the largest idol. And when Terah returned and saw the broken idols' pieces on the floor, he accused Abraham. But Abraham said to his father that the largest of the idols had killed all of the others in a fight over an offering brought to them. His father said it was impossible because those idols were made out of stones and wood; they had no life in them. And Abraham answered his father by saying, 'If they have no life in them, then why do they worship them?'"

Sissy stated, "This was a story that was taken from a Jewish Bible. Mariah Guerard's father was Jewish. He told the story to Mariah when she was a little girl growing up in Bluffton, South Carolina. Mariah passed the story down to her children and grandchildren, and I passed the story down to my children and grandchildren." In the story, Sissy was telling us that there is only one living God, and He has control over everything.

Sissy believed in telling real-life stories, because it was the best way to pass information about many things that she wanted us to know about spirits, God, and family. She also told us many stories about the King family's history. She told us that her family home sat on 1,960 acres of land south of Hampton River off southeast Georgia along the south Atlantic coastal area. That tract of land was called South Hampton Plantation. Later, the name changed to South Hampton Island, which is now part of South Hampton Preserve.

Sissy looked at her grandchildren with proud eyes and proclaimed, "I was born and raised on South Hampton Island, Georgia, as of all of my grandmother Mariah's children and grandchildren. Mariah Guerard was my grandmama. I remembered her to be a short, fat but beautiful woman.

The Forgotten Kings

I want y'all to always remember this." And she would continue, "Y'all are the Black descendants of Roswell King Sr. He was my great-great granddaddy. Roswell King Jr. was my great-granddaddy. And Roswell King III was my granddaddy. Roswell III was called Rossie or Ross. Go to the library and look up the King family history. The Kings are some wealthy, powerful, and famous people. And they got something for y'all, but now is not the time. Now don't y'all go talk these things, 'cause they'll lynch y'all."

Roswell King III portrait.

Mariah Guerard portrait.

What did Sissy mean by stating, "And they got something for y'all"? Sissy was referring to a will written by her granddaddy Roswell III to his Black family in coastal Georgia. Roswell III verbally told Mariah that he had a written will for her and their family. The written will bequeathed his whole King inheritance to go to Mariah and their children when he died. However, Mariah, her children, and the rest of her generation never obtained a copy of the will written by Roswell III because it was kept away from them.

Sissy passed the information about the land in South Hampton Island, and Roswell III's will, down to her children and grandchildren. She mentioned, "Before he died in September 1911, he told the love of his life, Mariah, that he wrote a will for her and their children. It awarded all of his inheritance to go to her family when he died."

Although Mariah, her children, and her grandchildren knew about the will, they were afraid to pursue it over the years. Mariah and her family believed wholeheartedly it would be a horrendous massacre among the family if they pursued Roswell III's will. The white members of the King family did not want Mariah and her family to have any of Roswell III's inheritance under any circumstances. So the other family members deliberately kept the will away from Mariah, her family, and from Liberty County, Georgia.

A title search in Liberty County courthouse records shows the copy of the will never reached Liberty County. It was believed to include a living trust, estates, properties, shares of stocks, and other hidden treasures.

Roswell III was a man who lived in two worlds—one white family and one Black family—but chose to dedicate the remainder of his life to his Black family in coastal Georgia. Mariah and her children were never accepted by the King family. They were what we know today as mixed-race. But in the Southern states during the slavery era, they were known as mulattoes. Mariah and her children were considered to be mulattoes. This is an admixture of Indians, Jewish, and Caucasians. And her grandchildren were an admixture of African-Americans. In the eyes of the King family members, the mulatto family members were outcasts and did not belong as a part of the Kings' family heritage.

Mariah and her children were too white to be Black and too Black to be white. Meaning that their skin tones were white-skinned in color like Caucasians, but their innocent blood was a mixture of another race. Because they were mulattoes, they were not allowed to attend public schools with the white race. And because their skin tones were Caucasians, they were not allowed to attend public schools with the Black race. To ensure Mariah's children were educated, she homeschooled all of them.

The stories told by Sissy of her grandfather Roswell III's will, and the tract of land at South Hampton Island, were also told by Eva (King, later Cook) Jones. Eva was Sissy's aunt. She was the daughter of Roswell III and Mariah. Aunt Eva told a more in-depth, detailed history of her family. She too warned the family to stay away from Roswell III's will and the land at South Hampton Island. I recall her saying, "Now don't y'all go back there, because it ain't the time! Leave it alone! Those people will kill y'all!" Aunt Eva also was afraid of what would happen to us if the Black King family members tried to regain the land at South Hampton Island, or even pursue the content in the will of her father, Roswell King III. Can you imagine the fear they felt believing that they would be killed?

As I reflect upon the words that Sissy and Aunt Eva said—"They'll lynch y'all" and "Those people will kill y'all"—they may have seemed a little harsh to say to young children, but they were afraid for our lives if we tried to claim the inheritance that Roswell King III left us. They truly believed in their hearts that if any of their family members ever pursued the will or the land at South Hampton Island, the threats would be so real for the Black King family in coastal Georgia. In those days, there was no way the King family members would ever have allowed the inheritance of Roswell III to go to Mariah and her children. So Mariah and her family remained silent for fear of being harmed, or yet worse, their lives being taken.

Mariah and her family lived in the deep south during the peak of high racial disparity in the late 1800s and early 1900s. The ferociousness and hatred toward Blacks were still lingering, and torment was running rampant in the southern towns. From the time when the United States abolished slavery in 1863 to the time the civil rights movement began in 1955 when

Rosa Parks was arrested for refusing to move to the back of the bus, civil rights were not even merely a concept or thought in people's minds. During this era, there was not a single African-American policeman in the five deep southern states. The poverty rate for Black families was a staggering 87 percent. Jim Crow was alive in the southern states. Also in the southern states, criminal activities were accepted for terror and revenge. In fact, any white person could strike or beat a Black person, steal or destroy his property or land, cheat him in a transaction, and even take his life without much fear of legal action.

One of the most profound events that occurred in Sissy's childhood took place when she was a little girl around thirteen years old. It was a life-changing experience. After the death of Roswell III in September 1911, his second family continued to live on South Hampton Island for thirteen years.

On August 4, 13, 19, and 26, 1924, notices were published in Savannah's newspaper once a week for four weeks preceding the sale of the land, by order of the sheriff of Liberty County, Georgia. The sale of land on South Hampton Island was wrongly sold by the King's family members. So they plotted against the heirs of Roswell III. They did not intend for Roswell III's second family to receive any land or estate of his inheritance.

On one sultry summer afternoon in September 1924, Mariah Guerard, her children, and her grandchildren were run off the 1,960 acres of South Hampton Island. Sissy told a life story of the time when it happened. She remembered it like it happened yesterday. While telling the story, I could hear it in her voice that she still felt a little unease about the event that had happened more than fifty years earlier. With slight anxiety in her tone of voice, she stated, "I was a little girl about thirteen years old. I was sitting on the swing under the big oak tree near the family big house playing with my brothers and sisters."

Next to the big house on South Hampton Island was a large oak tree, one of the oldest and the largest trees on the plantation. The oak tree was where they played around during the hot days. A swing was built and hung from one of the limbs, which was made from two huge, twisted natural-fiber ropes that were tied to each end of a four-by-eight-inch board. The Kings' children and grandchildren played on the swing as youngsters. Even though the swing is no longer there, the rope is tied around the limb and remains embedded for more than one hundred years. The oak tree is still standing today and became a landmark for where Roswell King's South Hampton Plantation house, and the grave yard were once located. Although the house has been torn down, the foundation is still there, as well as the unmarked graves.

Sissy shook her head and said, "We noticed white men coming to the house in a vehicle. The men got out of the vehicle and walked up to the front door of the big house. They called for Mariah to come outside. In a state of paranoia, Mariah and my father, Hardee, came to the door and asked, 'What do you want?' With guns in hand, the men told Mariah and Hardee, 'This land has been sold. South Hampton Island no longer belongs to you."

The big house on South Hampton had fifteen people living in it. The members of the household were Mariah, her sons, daughters, daughter-in-law, and grandchildren. Mariah lived at Roswell King's South Hampton Island for more than fifty-three years, until they were driven off the land in September 1924. The family had no idea the land had been sold. The land was supposedly sold by the Kings' other family members without the knowledge of Mariah and her family.

Sissy continued, "They gave us until sunset to get off the land on South Hampton Island." Of course Mariah and Hardee refused them, but with guns drawn and pointed at them, the threat seemed too real. Just in case Mariah and Hardee were not taking their demands seriously, the men compellingly reiterated to get off of the land. And the men said once more in a stern voice, "We're giving you until sunset to get off the land before we return." Then the men got back into the vehicle and left.

Mariah was a strong woman and the head of the household at the time. Furious beyond measure, she gathered her family members together near the big oak tree and explained what was happening. Then she gave everyone his and her responsibility to get all of their belonging off the land before sunset. The family was running out of time. And they couldn't come back the next day, and time was ticking. They had to get all of their possessions packed up and moved in one trip, because they were forbidden to set foot back on that land ever again, or there would be serious consequences.

Sissy stated, "Everyone was instructed to pitch in, and to do their part in loading the wagon for the move. The King family didn't have a vehicle for the move, so we began to gather up all of our belongings and packed everything up onto the wagon." Their main means of transportation was by mule and wagon. She said, "The wagon was loaded to the capacity with clothes, furniture, household items, cooking utensils, and farm tools. Everything we could carry out of the house was put onto one wagon; it almost stood ten feet high. And the items near the sides were hanging so low off the wagon, they almost touched the ground."

Mariah Guerard's daughters, Rosa King, Eva King, and Mariah King, were in charge of gathering the children and getting all of their items out of the house.

Sissy described the Kings' house in South Hampton Island to be a huge white wooded house with four fireplaces. Each fireplace had two sides. They were built between the walls that separated two rooms; that way a fireplace opening was accessible to each of the eight different rooms in the house. This allowed all the rooms of the house to be heated during those cold winter days and nights.

Sissy further explained how the wagon was loaded, and how they escaped before the men returned at the end of the day. "The wagon was all loaded with the belongings in the big house, but there was one last item that Mariah needed to get out of the house. She went to her bedroom and located a wooded chest that was in the corner of her bedroom floor. She opened it. And there it was—a chest full of money that she and Roswell III had been saving over the years. Not all of the family money was placed in the bank. No one ever knew just how much money was in that chest, but it was surely enough money to start a new life elsewhere. Time was running out before the men would return. So my grandmother, Mariah, began to grab handfuls of money and started stuffing as much of it as possible into her dress areas. The money was even sticking out the top of her dress. It was too much money to carry by hand. And the remaining money in the chest was gathered by my daddy Hardee and uncle Eddie. They had to gather up the remaining money and place it in sheets and wrapped it up. There was no more room on the wagon for the chest."

Sissy explained the other responsibilities to Hardee and Eddie. "They were in charge of the farm animals and transporting everything." The men gathered the cows, chicken, mules, and farm tools for the move. They had to move it all from South Hampton Island to Chapman. Chapman was located about five miles west of the South Hampton Island home. Sissy stated, "With the mules in place and the wagon loaded with our belongings, we began our tedious journey." The children, grandchildren, and farm animals trailed the wagon on foot down the dusty dirt road through the wooded area to Chapman. She added, "We escaped just before the white men returned before sunset." Mariah's heart was beating a mile a minute from the adrenaline she felt while trying to get her family off of the land before sunset. It took her some time to recover. This event had shaken her to her core.

My grandmother Sissy never mentioned who the men were that came to the house. And Mariah knew it was not any members of Roswell King III's other family, since they knew all of their faces. And they would not have wanted to cause any physical harm to any of them. I suspect the men were from the lumber company that the land was sold to in August 1924, along with the Sheriff.

The King family was forced from the wonders of South Hampton Island and started a new life in a different place. Mariah and her family moved in with family members in the Chapman community until they can establish their own homes. The new life brought about new challenges for Roswell King III's second family.

With the money Mariah got from the chest in her bedroom in South Hampton Island, she was able to purchase a large tract of land in the Chapman community totaling 110 acres deeded to Hardee King. The deed to the land can be found in the Liberty County, Georgia, courthouse. Mariah had homes built for her and her surviving children. She bought supplies for Hardee and Eddie King to build homes. And enough supplies to build homes for her daughters Eva and Rosa King. She also bought a house in Savannah, Georgia, for her daughter Mariah King.

Sons Hardee and Eddie were very skilled in carpentry like their father. They were the primary builders of the homes in Chapman. These houses were uniquely designed. The inner frameworks of the houses were made out of logs, such as a log cabin with two mutually orthogonal walls meeting at the corners. The logs were made from trees that were cut down on their property. They bought flat pieces of wooden boards and shingles for the external walls of the house to protect it against the elements and to help provide support. They also used boards on the internal walls of the house to beautify them. The floor and ceiling were also made out of boards. The roofing of the house was made of steel roofing sheets. Most houses in the early part of the twentieth century had metal roofing, mainly because metal did not burn, which helped prevent house fires caused by chimneys and stovepipes.

The homes built for the King family in Chapman had no running water, no electricity, and no in-house toilets. The family got water from a local well. Oil lamps and candles were used for lighting. They used an outhouse for their toilet, which was built a short distance from the main house. Each house had a fireplace for heating during the cold winter season.

The kitchen shed and living areas were also built separately from the main house. Mainly because, if a fire were to occur in the kitchen shed, it would not burn down the living area. The stove they used was an old cast-iron stove. It served a dual purpose in the winter months for cooking and heating. The kitchen shed was also made from steel roofing sheets. This would prevent hot coals and ashes from the cast-iron stove from starting a fire on the roof. Building and buying homes were the first steps in the life of Mariah's family they had to endure after relocating from the land they were driven off.

This picture of House 1 was taken in September 2004. It was built in 1924 by the King's men after the King's family was run off the land in South Hampton Island. The building on the left is the main house. The small building on the right is the kitchen shed. Shingles were used on the external walls. Metal roofing sheets were used to prevent house fires caused by chimneys.

This picture shows the type of shingles used on House 1 external walls.

This picture of House 2 was taken in May 2014. It was also built in 1924 by the King's men. Logs were used on the inner framework. Boards were used on the external walls. Metal roofing sheets were used on the roof.

This picture is the inside view of a wall. It shows the type of logs used on House 1 and House 2 inner framework.

Chapter 2

The Generations of Roswell King

There was once this wealthy, powerful, and infamous man who died during the mid-1840s and left an inheritance to his family. But before his death, this powerful and successful man, along with his sons, were supporters of slavery. This man's name was Roswell King Sr. This particular son of an Irish immigrant was an exceedingly strong-willed, clever, educated, business-minded, and creatively cruel man.

Roswell Sr. was the son of Thomas "Captain Timothy" King, a weaver and Revolutionary naval commander. Thomas King was married to Sarah Anne Fitch. She was a direct descendant of John Fitch of Fitch Castle of Essex, England, and the sister of John Fitch, the inventor of the steamboat.

These storylines will give brief descriptions and backgrounds of three particular namesake descendants of Thomas King. The namesake's history began with Roswell King Sr., the father; Roswell King Jr., the son; and Roswell King III, also known as Rossie or Ross, the grandson, and how these men interacted with society.

I. These are the Generations of Thomas "Captain Timothy" King (1579-1586):[1]

Thomas "Captain Timothy" King (1727–1812), and Sarah Anne Fitch (1736–1785) were the dynasties of the Kings' lineage. Together, they had eleven children, and three preceded them in death. These are the names of their children: George King married Tryphena Latimer. Timothy King died as a child at three years old. Reuben King died early in childhood. Sarah King married Aaron Bates. Renamed son Timothy King died at two years old. Roswell King Sr. (1765–1844) married Catherine Barrington (1776–1839). Merriam King married Solomon Allen. Thomas King married Sarah Meers. Abigail (Nabby or Gabby) King married Isaac Hunt. The linear renamed son Timothy King never married. And a planar renamed son Reuben King married Abigail Austin.

Thomas and Sarah King's son Roswell Sr. grew up to be an entrepreneur, a great business-mind but yet a cruel man. He was born on May 3, 1765, in Windsor, Connecticut. When Roswell Sr. was twenty-three, he pursued a fresh start and set out to make a new life in southeast coastal Georgia. Later, he became a slave owner in Georgia. There he met and married Catherine Barrington in 1792 in the town of Darien in southeast coastal Georgia, where they resided. She was the daughter of Lieutenant Colonel Josiah Barrington of England and a relative of General James Oglethorpe, the founder of the state of Georgia in 1733.

II. These are the generations of Roswell King Sr. (1579-1586):[2]

Roswell King Sr. and his wife, Catherine (Barrington) King had ten children. Three preceded them in death. These are the names of their children: Son Rufus King died at the age of fourteen. His namesake was son Roswell King Jr. (1796–1854), a slave owner in southeast coastal Georgia who married Julia Rebecca Maxwell (1808–1892). Son Barrington King was a shrewd businessman and the co-founder of the city of Roswell, Georgia, and he married Catherine Margaret Nephew. Daughter Catherine King died in early childhood. Son Ralph King married Isabella Gibbs and later married Mildred. Son Thomas King married Jane Bryde. Son William King married Sarah Elizabeth McLeod. Son Pierce Butler King was named after Major Pierce Butler, one of the largest slaveholders in Georgia, and died as a baby. Daughter Elizabeth Barrington King married Nicholas Baynard. And the renamed daughter, Catherine Barrington King, married Reverend Nathaniel Alpheus Pratt of Savannah, Georgia.

From 1793 to 1802, Roswell Sr.'s earlier occupation in southeast coastal Georgia included jobs as a surveyor in Glynn County, justice of the peace in McIntosh County, Glynn County representative to the Georgia House of Representatives, and lumber measurer. He was also a business owner in Darien, where he built structures made of tabby. Tabby is a type of concrete made with a mixture of shells, lime, and water. Roswell Sr. was the owner of the Darien Bank in Darien, Georgia, one of the strongest in the South at that time. He also owned two thousand acres of tracts of land located in Glynn County, Georgia.

From 1802 to 1820, Roswell Sr. managed rice and cotton on two of Major Pierce Butler's slave plantations in southern coastal Georgia. Major Pierce Butler was an Irish immigrant who became an officer in the Revolutionary War and later became the United States senator of South Carolina. He was also one of the largest slave owners in South Georgia, where he owned about five hundred slaves. Roswell Sr. lived and worked on both of Butler's plantations. Later, he used exponential business-management skills to own and manage his slave plantation in Darien, Georgia. Roswell Sr. was very educated, experienced, and exceptional as a businessman, rice planter, and entrepreneur.

In 1828 gold was found in north Georgia, which caused settlers to travel to this territory. As a perceptive businessman, Roswell Sr. left Darien to investigate the gold-infested region. Leaving his wife behind in Darien, he journeyed on horseback to the Chattahoochee River near what is now called the city of Roswell, Georgia. To maximize his potential of being proactive and not reactive, Roswell Sr. took thirty-six slaves from his plantation along with him. The slaves were used as labor to construct a textile mill and help build the town of Roswell, Georgia.

Before construction began on this rich land near the Chattahoochee River, the land was inhabited by Cherokee Indians. The Native Americans were resistant to giving up their territory, but they were eventually driven off their land. Once the Native Americans were forced out, Roswell Sr. hauled in more slaves and used them as laborers to work and help clear the land.

Roswell King Sr. had homes built for himself and his family and built apartments for mill workers, a general store, a church, and an academy for children. He also purchased an additional forty-two slaves in Darien for approximately $22,000 and transported them to Cobb County, now Fulton County, to help with the buildings. His son Barrington King joined him and offered investment opportunities to his other family members, and a city was built near the Chattahoochee River.

In 1838 Roswell Sr. began work on his first cotton mill as one of the pioneers in the industry. One year later, he incorporated his empire and named it the Roswell Manufacturing Company. The company was extremely successful and very profitable. Unfortunately, Roswell Sr.'s wife, Catherine (Barrington) King, did not partake in his booming legacy. She never laid eyes on the empire her husband created in a city named after him. She died in 1839 and was buried in the Historic Midway Cemetery in Liberty County, Georgia. On February 15, 1844, Roswell King Sr. died and was buried in the Old Cemetery in Roswell, Georgia.

Before the death of Roswell King Sr. and Catherine (Barrington) King, their second child and namesake to his father, Roswell King Jr., was his father's right-hand man in coastal Georgia. Roswell King Jr. was born on April 2, 1796. Although Roswell Jr. was born in Savannah, Georgia, he spent most of his adult life as a plantation manager of Major Pierce Butler's rice and cotton plantations, jointly with his father, Roswell Sr. The rice cultivation on the plantation was a very lucrative business in the low country along with Georgia's coastal lands.

Roswell Sr. left to settle in northern Georgia in 1820. His son, Roswell Jr., at the age of twenty-four, took over his father's reign as Major Pierce Butler's plantation manager from 1820 to 1838. Roswell Jr. inherited and emulated supreme management skills from his father. After managing the plantation for Mr. Butler, Roswell Jr. decided to manage his plantation. In 1838 he bought the South Hampton Plantation, also called South Hampton Island. For $22,000 Roswell Jr. bought forty-two slaves from his brother Barrington King to work on his plantation.

III. Slavery in Liberty County:

Liberty County became a county in coastal Georgia in 1777, during the Revolutionary War. The first settlers did not arrive until the early part of the 1750s. The oldest town in Liberty County is Riceboro, Georgia, located in the southern coastal region of Georgia. It has many waterways and was their primary source of transportation—by way of canoes through the many winding rivers and out to the islands.

Riceboro was the center of the political and commercial activities in the county. It was called the Borough for short. Rice was the premier crop grown in the area. Later the spelling was changed from Riceborough to the present name Riceboro.

The major agricultural crop in coastal Georgia during the 1800s was rice. Slaves from West Africa, mainly from the Casamance region, were captured and brought to America to cultivate rice in the southern coastal states. Slaves from the Casamance region were experienced and skilled in growing rice. They brought technology and knowledge about rice with them to the rice fields in coastal South Carolina and coastal Georgia.

Slaves were used as cheap labor to work on the American slave plantations. There were many dangers associated with that life—many of which we'll discuss later in this chapter—but one I want to highlight is malaria, which was exceptionally dangerous for everyone but especially slaves. Working in the rice fields required a lot of standing water, and the lowline still waters of the swamps were the perfect condition for the breeding grounds of mosquitoes, which often carried malaria. It was also a belief that bad air from the unwholesome air in swampy districts also caused the disease.

Many whites were able to be treated by doctors, but slaves had to develop their home remedies from local plants, including herbs, herbal teas, sage, tree barks, other plants, and other natural cures from the earth. Fatback from a pig was used to draw poison from the body. Tea leaves made from herbs were used to reduce fever. The tree barks were used to strengthen teeth. Salt from the salty rivers was used for infections. And eating garlic was used to help reduce swelling.

Another life-threatening condition that occurred in the swampy waters of the rice fields was the danger of mysteriously surfaced alligators and deadly poisonous rattlesnakes, water moccasins, and copperheads, all belonging to the pit viper snake class. Bites from these snakes can inject enough poison to kill a fully grown human in hours and indeed kill many whites, slaves, and Native Americans. The venomous snakes lived mostly in low-elevation areas of the riverbanks, marshland, and warm swamps, thereby making the rice fields an excellent place for attack. These dangerous conditions obliterated the lives of the people who lived and farmed the dangerous terrain.

In general, life as a slave in coastal Georgia during the slavery days was a hard knock. Not only did the cruel and unjust punishment of slave owners take their lives, but other means of danger lurked waiting for them. As mentioned, for example, malaria and other diseases were rampant. These diseases took the lives of both slaves and hired help, such as the Native Americans. Native Americans also worked on rice plantations. The Creek Indians and Cherokee Indians were not slaves but worked along with the slaves to help on the plantation to harvest rice and to manufacture salt from water from the salty Hampton River inlet. Many Native Americans in our colonial history contributed to the building of the South. The Creek and Cherokee Indians are Native American people traditionally from the southeastern United States, including Georgia and South Carolina.

In addition to mistreatment, disease, and other risks regularly faced by slaves, there was another tragic event that took place in the mid-1800s that also destroyed many enslaved families. This event occurred in 1859 during the largest slave sale ever recorded in the history of the United States which occurred over two days at the racetrack in Savannah, Georgia.

Major Pierce Butler owned approximately nine hundred slaves. Mr. Butler was deeply in debt and had to satisfy his creditors. He sold off almost half of his slaves, so some 436 men, women, and children were auctioned off from his Butler Island and South Hampton plantation, near Darien, Georgia. This huge breakup of families and homes after the sale was known and remembered as 'The Weeping Time'.

Map of Coastal Georgia drawing.

Slave families were divided and broken beyond repair. There were numerous days of sorrow, heartache, weeping, and crying. Hundreds of slaves were uprooted and permanently placed in new environments with only a distant memory of the warmth of a loved one. They were never to reunite with their families; parents were separated from their children, and married couples from each other.

The most humane thing to do to an enslaved family was to sell them as one unit, but that was not always the case. It depended on the requests of the slave buyers, the purchasing power of their dollars, and the labor force needed on the farms and plantations that forced them to buy slaves individually. Some slaves tried to plea to the prospective buyers to purchase them as an entire family. Babies as young as three months old were sold without their parents that day.

Can you imagine being ripped away from your mother, father, siblings, or even your children? That would be devastating to any human being. This was one of the darkest times ever in African-American heritage; the fourth generation was removed from slavery and hundreds of slaves lost their families and their heritage. Slaves were sold off throughout the deep south as far north as Virginia and as far west as Mississippi.

During the slavery era, sometimes it was hard to trace African-American slaves. Slave ownership would be made public, but on a few occasions, they would be kept as private records. Slaves were not recorded on vital records. Their family information was only available from their former owners' records. The key is to learn as much as possible about the owner and his family because the slaves were considered the property of the slave owners. They were listed under the name of the owner, each slave only by sex, specific age, and color. The slave family information was also passed down by word of mouth or oral storytelling, like in the book *Roots*.

These are the generations of Roswell King Jr.:

Roswell King Jr. and his wife, Julia Rebecca Maxwell, had eleven children. These are the names of their children: Mary Elizabeth King married Dr. Charlton Henry Wells. James Audley Maxwell King married Elizabeth Catherine "Kate" Lewis. George Frederick "Fred" King was never married. William "Willie" Henry King was also never married. And his namesake Roswell King III, his mother's favorite child, married Catherine "Kitty" Ashmead (1842–1872).[3] Roswell III and Catherine had six children.

The sixth in this union was Isabel Cooper King, who married Mathews Robert Tunno. Julian Clarence King was the seventh child, and he married Georgia Barrington Anderson. Their eighth child was Bayard Hand King, and he married Fernanda Madrill. John "Johnnie" Butler King was the ninth child, and he married Mary Agnes Battey. Last, there were two other children born into this union, but they died during early childhood.

Roswell Jr. later moved from South Hampton Plantation to Woodville, Georgia. Roswell Jr. died on July 1, 1854. Before his death, he wrote a last will and testament, but the will was not dated until April 1880, twenty-six years after his death. Roswell Jr.'s nephew Reverend Charles B. King, the son of his brother Barrington King, was the administrator of Roswell Jr.'s will. Roswell Jr.'s wife, Julia, died on Colonel's Island, Georgia, in 1892. Both were buried at Midway Cemetery in Midway, Georgia.

Notoriously historians have documented that both father and son, Roswell King Sr. and Roswell King Jr., were cruel slave masters. A journalist at the *Atlanta Journal-Constitution* once wrote articles in the newspaper about Roswell Sr. One of the famous column entries written in November 1991 was titled "The Harrowing Career of Roswell King." The writer described Roswell Sr. to be a ruthless and unjust man toward his slaves. The writer was saddened and even embarrassed about how Roswell Sr. treated his slaves.

Roswell Sr. spoke of African slaves as if they were animals, and he justified the sadistic behaviors toward slaves were justifiable. Stories have been told that Roswell Sr. once made an enslaved man walk from Savannah, Georgia, to his plantation in coastal Georgia on a broken foot. Often slave owners inflicted merciless treatment upon their slaves to terrorize them with fear, thereby eliminating any chances of slaves running away or revolting.

Similar to Roswell Sr. as a slave owner, most slave owners believed slaves did not deserve equal rights. Even the state delegates in the United States Constitutional Convention in 1787 came up with a three-fifths compromise on how slaves were to be counted when determining a state's population. The compromise-determining fact was to count three out of every five slaves a person. Some argued that slaves were zero-fifths of a man, meaning they proclaimed slaves were not human at all.

As a collective, some white slave owners from the South believed that slaves were constitutionally, intellectually, and morally inferior to whites. They deemed slavery to be justifiable and socially acceptable. Since slavery is mentioned in the Bible, and the Bible is God's words, they believed God condones slavery, and God is an advocate of slavery. Therefore, the slave owners felt they had every right to punish and treat their slaves cruelly or inhumanely. They felt they could do whatever they wanted to their slaves because they considered slaves to be their property.

IV. Christianity and Slaves' Genealogy:

In the fourth century, in the year 325 AD, the biblical text was tremendously edited. At least forty-five books were completely taken away, or exceedingly edited into the Bible we know today. And we lost a tremendous amount of information. The Roman emperor Constantine the Great was the first to convert to Christianity. Constantine, with the early Christian Bible, had to decide what information to include and what information to exclude from the Bible. We know some of the biblical text was lost because we can recover the information in the Dead Sea Scrolls, noncanonical books, and the Coptic text.

By the year 404 AD, most books of the Bible were translated into English. This translation forms the basis of the Latin Bible that would be used for most of the Middle Ages. This was later translated into the English-language version in 1382.

By 1611 there were eighty books in the Bible when it was translated from Latin to English. And in the year 1684, the Vatican removed fourteen books from the Bible making up the sixty-six books we know today. But for whatever reason, the Catholic church chose to remove them from the Bible. Some may believe, perhaps, the content of the books removed did not fit in with the Roman Catholic church's chronicle. And some may believe, perhaps, that the word of God would read exactly what they wanted it to be. No one knows for sure.

Christianity has played an important role in shaping American religion and culture. Slave owners used religion to control their slaves. Christianity's Bible verses taught slaves to obey their earthly masters. A Presbyterian pastor of Liberty County, Georgia, Charles Colcock Jones Sr. (1804–1863), wrote many papers and books about slaves and religion. He was known as the Apostle to Slaves. In 1842 Pastor Charles Jones Sr. wrote a particular book on slaves and religion titled *The Religious Instruction of the Negroes in the United States*. This book appealed to slave owners and ministers who wanted to give religious guidance to slaves. The table of contents showed the book had four parts. Part I gives the *Historical Sketch of the religious Instruction of the Negroes*. Part II gives *The Moral and the Religious Condition of the Negroes in the United States*. Part III gives the *Obligations of the Church of Christ to Attempt the Improvement of the Moral and Religious Condition of the Negroes in the United States*. And Part IV gives the *Means and Plans for Promoting and securing the Religious Instruction of the Negroes in the United States*.[4]

Pastor Charles Jones Sr. believed that Negro slaves lacked virtue as if they didn't have souls, and described Negroes to be ignorant of Christianity (Jones 1842, 52,58). He mentioned that Negroes are the most degraded of all people on the earth (Jones 1842, 64). And because of their lack of character and immoral behaviors, slaves were totally dependent on white men for the ability to overcome their limitations (Jones 1842, 81). He also wrote in his book that Negroes marriages are not recognized nor protected by the law (Jones 1842, 68). Negroes husband or wife may be divided at any time by the owner such as debt, sale, or during difficult times by the owner. Pastor Charles Jones Sr. was a slave owner as well. He supervised three plantations—Montevideo, Arcadia, and Maybank—all while continuing his evangelization of slaves. His slave plantations are documented in the Midway Museum in Midway, Georgia.

During the slavery era, sometimes it was difficult to trace African-American slaves' genealogy. Most slave owners would make their slave records public, but others would keep them as private records. Since slaves' births and deaths were not recorded on vital records, only familial documents or ledgers were retrievable from previous slave owners. As a matter of fact, slaves were listed as property under the name of the owner by gender, first name, age, and skin color.

The overall question to ask is, why do slave owners hate African slaves? This is a deep-rooted question that has been asked for hundreds of years, perhaps since the beginning of mankind. The slave owners believed they were the superior race or the master race. They furthermore believed all humans derived from the white race.

Anatomists have evidence that the oldest known human fossils were found in North Africa, which is a region of dark-skinned people. The land we know today as Israel, a Middle Eastern country on the Mediterranean Sea, was once a region of dark-skinned people. For thousands of years, Israelites migrated to different parts of the world.

Most Christians do not want to believe Jesus was of the dark-skinned race. Biblical scholars wrote that Jesus was born in Bethlehem, a city in Israel. After the golden age, the land of Israel was divided into two kingdoms during the ninth century: the Kingdom of Israel and the Kingdom of Judah. Both were dark-skinned regions in the Middle East. That Middle Eastern region of land was divided into twelve tribes. They were the traditional kin group among the ancient Israelites. The twelve tribes of Israel descended from the twelve sons of Jacob. The Tribe of Judah was one of the twelve Tribes of Israel. Jesus was born a dark-skinned Israelite and a member of the Tribe of Judah.

The Tribes of Israel were scattered among the Nations, and some migrated to West Africa. The West Africans are believed to be the true Hebrew Israelites. The people did not obey all of God's commands and kept that covenant. Because of this belief, some people think that Blacks were cursed and became the most hated people of all time. The children of Israel would suffer under constant oppression and harsh treatment.

In the Bible, the book of Deuteronomy, chapter 28, talks about blessings and curses. Verses 1 through 14 deal with blessings. And the remaining fifty-four verses, 15 through 68, deal with curses. Chapter 28 tells of the blessings and curses of the Twelve Tribes of Israel. The basic cause of blessings comes from listening diligently to the voice of God and doing what He says, which will result in God's favor. The basic cause of curses comes from not listening to the voice of God and not doing what He says, which results in God's disfavor.

If the people of Israel had kept the covenant, they would have remained in God's favor throughout all time and would not have suffered the curses that came with it. Because of the people's disobedience, the Bible states they will be sold into slavery and scattered among all the nations from one end of the earth to the other. They have become the Lost Tribes of Israel. And in those nations, they will find no peace or place to rest until God shows them favor once more. These are the dark-skinned Israelites.

Furthermore, Tacitus is a Roman historian, who likens Jews to having Egyptian origin. Strabo, a Greek historian, likens the Jews to an Ethiopian origin. So there we have two historians, Greek and Roman, who state the people from the regions where Jesus was from were dark-skinned in complexion and of African origin.

A slave is not an immigrant, nor is a slave a servant. Being a slave is far worse than being a servant. Slaves and servants are similar in a lot of ways. Both slaves and servants were people who were kidnapped or bought and sold to work. The difference between the two is most servants were people who worked for individuals with pay for a certain length of time. Once the time expired, they were freed. On the other hand, slaves were people who worked for individuals without pay. And they remained in slavery for life or until their freedom was bought. This was a common feature of the lives of African slaves in coastal Georgia and throughout the slave states.

V. Unjust Men toward Their Slaves:

During the time Roswell King Sr. and Roswell King Jr. were alive and owned slaves, they were known as malicious slave owners who brutally punished the slaves severely to control them. Additionally for the slaves who did not work hard enough or who sought to escape, punishments were vicious. Many of those slaves were whipped, hung (lynched), and subjected to other means of torture to evoke total submission to slavery. The purpose of the vicious treatment of African slaves was to break them from one form of life to another, to reduce them from their natural state in nature, destroy all will of the African slaves, reduce them to animalistic behaviors, and force them to comply with any demands, physical or emotional. And to simply set an example to others who may want to resist, stand up to them, run away, or otherwise not comply.

The terms *lynch*, *lynched*, *lynching*, and *lynch mob* were said to have been taken from the last name of a man named William Lynch. One of Lynch's torturous ways used to punish and control slaves was demonstrated by hanging. To strike fear into slaves, he would hang slaves in the open so other slaves could see the savagery of his punishment. William's brother, Charles Lynch, a slave owner in Lynchburg, Virginia, was reported during that period of colonial history; he and other Virginia planters were driving themselves into bankruptcy by torturing and killing so many of their slaves in their attempts to force Africans to submit to slavery.

While managing one of Major Pierce Butler's slave plantations, Roswell Jr. had conflicts with him on the Butler's Island Plantations over the treatment of slaves. Major Pierce Butler began to take a more reasonable approach to the treatment of slaves, mainly because of his wife, Fanny Kemble. Fanny was an abolitionist from the heart.

During her time in the South, Fanny lived four months on Butler plantation and St. Simons Island, Georgia, and wrote many journals about the cruelties of slavery. She wrote letters in her journal detailing the physical and sexual abuse, and other atrocities, imposed upon these enslaved men and women during her stay on the Butler plantation from 1838 to 1839. She utilized multiple resources in recording the slavery accounts primarily by self-witnessing, and by stories told by other slaves.

Fanny and Major Pierce Butler disagreed frequently over the mistreatment, living conditions, and handling of the slaves. Ultimately, she was the contributing factor that convinced him to be more liberal in feeding, clothing, and lodging his slaves as well as treating them reasonably.

Nevertheless, her reproach did not reach all slave owners. In some cases, enslaved African women were treated as sex slaves or bed wenches. Some slave owners, whether they were married or not, had long-term relations with their enslaved women. It was an understood "law" that slaves were seen as property, and they did not have the right or courage to resist these powerful men. Essentially many illegitimate babies were born and denied preferential treatment or freedom.

Most of the slave owners' wives knew about the adulterous affairs of their husbands. However, they publicly refused to acknowledge the fact that their husbands were impregnating enslaved women. The wives were defenseless and could not do or say anything about their husbands' behaviors. The slave owners' wives did not dare to confront their husbands for fear of being beaten or otherwise punished by their husbands for confronting them. Slave owners' wives were expected to be passive and obedient to their husbands; they were victims trapped in a world filled with pain and shame.

Nevertheless, the wives were morally and emotionally persecuted, and they rejected any hints of retaliation regardless of their repugnancies while being intimidated by the risk of losing wealth, prestige, and prominence but having no power. Unlike the enslaved women who were victimized physically or mentally, the wives were morally victimized and had to willingly or sometimes forcibly accept all that was happening.

The slave owners' wives had to "stay in their place" or as some would say "turn a blind eye" to their husbands' moral turpitude relentlessly. For the wives who did not earn any form of income, it would be impossible for them to survive with no support from their husbands.

Consequently, the wives had to constantly see the results of infidelity flaunted in their faces, the increasing numbers of mulatto children. The wives' fights were predominantly internal. The sly remarks and evil looks toward the female slaves along with the unremorseful behaviors of the slave owners did not compare to the mental anguish the wives experienced.

A mulatto is a person with one white parent and one Black parent, or more broadly, a person of mixed Black and white ancestry. Today, some reject the term *mulatto* because of its association with slavery and colonial and racial oppression, preferring terms such as *mixed, biracial, brown, Black,* and *African-American. Mulatto* may also refer to a mixture of Indians and African-Americans.

A mulatto person's skin tones were significantly lighter than those of the typical darker-skinned African slaves. It was obvious to everyone that the slave owners had fathered those mulatto children from their field slaves or house slaves or maids. It was a very common practice among many slave owners, including Roswell Sr. and Roswell Jr. As a result, there are documented cases in other books that claim Roswell Sr. and Roswell Jr. fathered many mulatto children by forcing themselves on enslaved women.

The mulatto children who were born to Roswell Sr. by his enslaved women remained in slavery throughout their lives. Unlike the children born to him by his wife, Catherine Barrington, they got the rewards of being a part of the King family heritage and received all the benefits from his wealth and prosperity.

Often we read about men in history who have taken enslaved women for their pleasure. I remember reading about one of the most notorious cases involving President Thomas Jefferson. Historians have stated that before and during his presidency of the United States, he had thirty-eight years of intimate relations with his slave Sally Hemings, and fathered six children with her. Throughout history, slave owners have used slave women to fulfill their sexual pleasures.

In 1828 Roswell King Sr. started a new life in Roswell, Georgia, after leaving his wife, Catherine, behind in Darien, Georgia. She lived in coastal Georgia for eleven years and not once visited the city of Roswell. During this period, it is apparent to me that Roswell Sr. had relations with enslaved women while living estranged from his wife.

Roswell Sr. and Roswell Jr. eventually left Major Pierce Butler's slave plantation in McIntosh County, Georgia. Meanwhile, the tentacles of slavery continued to brutalize and torment the souls of slaves near the coastal waters of Georgia.

Roswell Sr. left Darien, Georgia, and created a city and an empire near the Chattahoochee River in Georgia that still stands today. Meanwhile, Roswell Jr. carried on his father's legacy as a malevolent slave owner. Roswell Sr. created much wealth in the slave industry and banking, which became a gateway for other businesses. He was able to leave an enormous inheritance for the King family. The inheritance proceeded to several generations of King's descendants, including his sons, daughters, grandchildren, and great-grandchildren—all heirs to his wealth. This also was true for his grandson and namesake Roswell III.

VI. These are the generations of Roswell King III:

Roswell King III was the fifth child and namesake of his father, Roswell King Jr., and the grandson of Roswell King Sr. Roswell III was born in Hartford, Connecticut, on August 28, 1836. From 1854 to 1856, between the ages of eighteen and twenty, he worked in Cobb County, Georgia, about two miles outside the city of Roswell, Georgia, with his brother George Frederick King in the tannery business.[5] The tannery was a family trade that was passed down from their grandfather, Roswell Sr. However, Roswell III was a farmer like his father. Also, he inherited the craftiness of a shrewd business owner as a leading producer of salt in coastal Georgia, like his father.

In 1860, at the age of twenty-four, Roswell III married Catherine Ashmead from Philadelphia, Pennsylvania. They began their new life together in Liberty County, Georgia. During their marriage, they had six children in eleven years between 1861 and 1872. These are the names of their children: Gertrude King (born 1861), Frederick Wells King (born 1862), Carlton Henry King (born 1864), Georgia Rebecca King (born 1868), Roswell King IV (born 1870), and Bayard Ashmead King (born 1872). The names were given to me by Roswell Cook. He was the son of Eva (King) Cook, and the grandson of Roswell King III from his second family. The first three children were born in Walthourville, Georgia. The remaining three children were born on South Hampton Plantation.

A year after the marriage of Roswell III and Catherine, the American Civil War (1861–1865) was fought. This war was fought between the northern states, which was the Union, and several Southern slave states, which was the Confederacy. The Civil War was mainly about states' rights, federal authority, American western expansion, and slavery. Regrettably, this was the longest and bloodiest war ever fought on American soil.

Roswell III left his new family in November 1861 to serve in the Liberty Independence Army Troop during the Civil War for the Confederate states for four years, during which he served as a private with three of his brothers: George Frederick King, Bayard Hand King, and Julian Clarence King.[6]

The war took hundreds of thousands of soldiers' lives in the northern and southern states but mostly in the South. Roswell III fought throughout the war, observing horrific counts of death until he could not endure any more fighting and killing in war. He decided to go AWOL (absent without leave) from the Confederate Army.

Was Roswell III afraid of dying in the war? Did he have a different perspective on the war? Or was he becoming an abolitionist and thought the Civil War was wrong? Whatever the case, he was caught trying to escape. It was told by a family member of Roswell III that he was afraid of being in the war and simply was trying to escape. Roswell III was placed on trial, punished under NJP (non-judicial punishment), and sent to a military prison in the South. He was later released and discharged from the army. Other records show Roswell III surrendered at Hillsboro, North Carolina, in April 1865.

After leaving the military, he moved his family to Walthourville, Georgia, where he began farming. He failed miserably as a farmer and was brutalized by debt. He did not clear expenses at Walthourville, and his farm did not bring in profit while living there. He speaks of trying it one year longer, hoping to make money enough to buy a farm in the up country, out of Liberty County. In 1867 while still in debt, he and his family left his farm in Walthourville and took root at Roswell King's South Hampton Plantation in Liberty County, Georgia. That same year his mother, Julia Rebecca (Maxwell) King, and sister Mary Elizabeth (King) Wells, moved in with Roswell III and his wife to help them raise their children. Despite the new endeavor, his sister Mary died in 1871. She was buried on South Hampton Plantation.[7]

In 1872 Roswell III's wife, Catherine, died at the young age of thirty-six. Without the support of his wife, and after the death of his sister a year earlier, he was unable to take care of the children. The children's ages ranged from toddler to eleven years old. The young children were too much for his mother, Julia, to handle alone. Roswell III had no choice except to send his children to live with other family members. Resultantly, he sent his six children to live with his older brother, James Audley Maxwell King, and his wife, Elizabeth (Lewis) King, at what is now called Colonel's Island in Liberty County, Georgia.[8] James Audley Maxwell King was known by his middle name, Audley, by his family.

Audley and Elizabeth had four children of their own. Taking in his six nephews and nieces extracted difficult times for Audley and his family. He complained often about having so many mouths to feed now that he had a total of ten children in the household.[9] Undoubtedly, the stress became insurmountable at times. Roswell III's children lived on Colonel's Island, while he continued to live on Roswell King's South Hampton Plantation.

In 1880 his mother, Julia King, was the trustee of Roswell King's South Hampton Plantation, and had been ever since her husband, Roswell Jr., died in 1854. On April 1, 1880, Julia King signed a trust deed over to Roswell III, her favorite child.[10] This made him the new trustee of Roswell King's South Hampton Plantation. Julia lived with Roswell III for a while at the big house on the South Hampton Plantation and later moved to Colonel's Island, where she later died in 1892.

Now that Roswell III's wife and sister had passed away, and the children and mother had moved to live on Colonel's Island, he had to find someone to look after the house and take care of him. While his children were living with his brother and his wife, Roswell III started a new life with his second family around the year 1880.

Chapter 3

Roswell King III's Second Family's Lineage

Other books have disclosed the King family's culture and heritage. The books titled *Children of the Pride: A True Story of Georgia and the Civil War* and *Major Butler's Legacy: Five Generations of a Slaveholding Family* stated that after the death of Roswell King III's wife, Catherine King in 1872, he sent his six children to live in the household of his brother Audley King and his wife. In the books, it was documented that Roswell III had two families—one white family with his deceased wife, Catherine, and a second family who was Black.[11]

Mariah Guerard, a teenager at the time, worked for Roswell III at the South Hampton Plantation as his housemaid in the early 1880s. She became his housemaid, his helpmate. Later, the relationship turned from an employer-worker relationship into a love affair. Roswell III had everything he needed in a young mate. She was young, beautiful, and a good homemaker.

Roswell III was around forty-four years old when he and Mariah's relationship started in the early 1880s. He was a tall, slender man who stood about six feet three inches tall. His housemaid was a young, educated, and energetic woman who stood about five feet one inch.

Mariah Guerard was a mulatto, a mixture of Native American and Jewish ancestry. Her family originated from Bluffton, South Carolina.

Mariah's mother was a Cherokee Indian from South Carolina, and her father was a Jewish man from New York.

The misconception about Mariah is that other writers portray her to be of the Black race. We know now that is not true! Mariah's children were also considered to be mulattoes. Nowadays they are referred to as biracial, a mixture of white, Jewish, and Native American. Their children were not of African-American descent. They looked more like Caucasians, thus making it easy for them to pass as the white race. Nonetheless, the Black race in their family did not evolve until Roswell III, and Mariah's children married into the Black race and had children by African-Americans.

Roswell III and Catherine's children were born between the years 1861 and 1872. Roswell III and Mariah's first child was born in or around the year 1884. There was a fourteen-year span between the youngest child of Catherine and the oldest child of Mariah. All of Roswell III's and Mariah's children were born and raised on South Hampton Plantation. The 1910 Militia District 15, Liberty County, Georgia census data proved that Mariah Guerard, her children, and grandchildren lived together in the same South Hampton Plantation household.[12] The census listed the family race as Mulatto.

Roswell III was a good catch for Mariah. He was her security blanket and provided her with a good quality of life. He was, as one would say, her Boaz. Roswell III was much older than Mariah. It is very similar to the biblical story my grandmother told us about Boaz and Ruth in the Old Testament Bible. Mariah needed a home and security, as Ruth did. According to the Bible, Boaz and Ruth were married. After Boaz died, Ruth inherited all of Boaz's properties and possessions (Bible, Ruth chapters 2-3). The difference is that Mariah and her children did not receive Roswell III's properties and possessions after he died.

Ironically, the son of a slave owner, Roswell III, and his housemaid's life together was miscegenated. They were never legally married but lived as a common-law husband and wife and were deemed married without a marriage license. Even though he loved and cared for her, marriages between a white person or any non-white person were declared illegal in those days.

Anti-miscegenation laws banned any non-white from marrying a white person. According to Jim Crow Laws (1865), "Penalty for this misdemeanor that carried a fine between $200 and $500, or confinement in jail for three months, or both" (par. 6).[13]

Roswell III had done an unthinkable act by living together with a mulatto family. He went against his family's wishes and became the first of the King family to break the chain of racial inequality, and he saw his mulatto family as his equals.

The page had turned and a new chapter had begun in Roswell III's book of life with his new second family. Can you imagine what two of the deep south's most notorious slave owners, Roswell Sr. and Roswell Jr., would think if their descendants had a family with someone who was not white? And what would the two cruel slave owners feel about their son and grandson starting a family with a mulatto woman and leaving his inheritance to his Black family in coastal Georgia? They must be turning over in their graves knowing that their bloodline did the unthinkable, having a family with a non-white person.

Is this karma or what? As you sow, so shall you reap. What comes around goes around. The brutal slave owners' son and grandson had now taken a liking to a mulatto family. For years, these coastal slave plantation owners wickedly punished hundreds of slaves simply for not working hard enough or trying to escape slavery.

The slaves often felt the wrath of their whips for simply being Black and for the constant reminder of their submission to slavery. The King men had ripped away the innocence of fresh young women for their pleasures. Hopefully one day justice will somehow prevail for Mariah's family in coastal Georgia. Mariah Guerard was buried at Varnadoe Cemetery in 1938 near the Chapman community in Riceboro, Georgia.

Roswell King III was buried on South Hampton Plantation in September 1911.[14] The event was written in the family's Bible. It is believed that his body is still buried there. Sometime between 1924 and 1934, a marble marker was provided by the War Department for Roswell III inside the King's family burial plot in the Historical Midway Cemetery.

The marble marker reads, Roswell King CO G. 5 GA, CAV. C.S.A. The King's family members' burial plot is located in the back section of the cemetery inside a cemented *Roswell* wall.

My grandmother Annie (King) Wilkins, also known as Sissy, professed that she is the granddaughter of Roswell King III and Mariah Guerard. She has told life stories of how her grandparents met, and how the lineage of their family is traced through the King family. She explained, "My granddaddy Roswell III and Mariah had six children. All of them were born on the South Hampton Plantation." South Hampton Plantation was later named South Hampton Island. "My daddy's name is Hardee King. He was the firstborn, and the only child of Roswell III and Mariah that has offspring that are alive today." The names of Roswell III and Mariah's children are Hardee King, Eddie King, Rosa King, Eva King, Mariah King, and Marie King.

I. These are the untold stories of Roswell King III and Mariah Guerard's Children:

Hardee King (1884–1940) was born on South Hampton Island in Liberty County, Georgia, as the first of six children to Roswell King III and Mariah Guerard. In his youth, Hardee learned the skills of becoming a carpenter, handyman, and farmer, like his father. Hardee farmed vegetables such as peas, beans, and corn, and he also grew pecan trees and had a variety of fruit trees. His greatest agricultural pride was cultivating a huge vineyard of scuppernong white grapes, which he used to make jelly and wine. Hardee was the third generation of the Kings' lineage working in the family's business of producing salt.

Hardee married Rosa Quarterman after being romantically involved. Rosa was a tall, dark-skinned African-American woman with jet-black silky hair gliding down her back. Her ethnicity was a mixture of African-American and Cherokee Indian. The Quarterman family lived on the land across the Hampton River north of North Hampton Island in an area that was called Forty Acres. As a young man, Hardee would sometimes take a small boat or swim over to Forty Acres to engage in courtship with Rosa. The Quarterman family later moved to the Chapman community in Riceboro.

Where did the term "40 acres and a mule" come from? It derives from an order that General William Sherman issued during the war in 1865. According to Nadra Nittle,

"General Sherman led the Union Army forces through the south, marching through Georgia and the Carolinas. After his march to Savannah, Georgia, and the capture of Savannah, Sherman met with a group of Black ministers and asked them what do you want for your people? The Black ministers said to give them land. Let them be free and have land. Hearing the needs of the Black people, General Sherman issued Special Field Order, Number 15. He took all the land on the coast of Georgia and South Carolina's rice coast and divided it up into forty-acre plots for Black families. And Sherman said, we will also give you a mule. The army had lots of mules left over to provide for the families. This is how the origin of '40 acres and a mule' came to be. Hundreds, or maybe thousands, of Black families settled on Sherman's land; that is what they called it. This happened during the last few months of the Civil War. But later Andrew Johnson had all the Black families thrown off their forty-acre plots of land (par. 1,2,7,8)."[15]

Andrew Johnson was the 17th president of the United States. He assumed office after the assassination of President Abraham Lincoln in 1865. He grew up poor and considered himself a common man, but only when the common men were white. He was the first American president to be impeached, but he was not removed from office.

Hardee and his wife, Rosa, lived on South Hampton Island until the horrific event that took place in September 1924. This was when the Black King family members were run off their land. They were forced to start a new life in a strange area in the Chapman community in Riceboro, where new challenges erupted.

During the early 1900s through the Great Depression, the tentacles of poverty exploded in the United States. Times were hard. It was very difficult for men to find work and support their families, even for the King family.

Hardee was a handyman and a planter. But still, he had to find work to support his family. There were few jobs in Liberty County. Working in the woods as a pulpwood logger, or in the fields as a sharecropper, were the only jobs readily available. The closest job Hardee and his brother Eddie could find was in the town of Ludowici, Georgia, which was located miles away from their home.

Hardee worked in Ludowici delimbing trees. The term my grandmother used was *cut-dying*. This is a process of cutting down midsize yellow pine trees and removing the bark and small limbs from the trunk of the tree. After stripping the tree trunks of their bark and limbs, they were then cut to length to make electrical and telephone poles.

The tool used for cutting down trees was a two-man crosscut saw. The saw had a wooden handle on each end, and one side pulled the handle while the other side pushed the handle. The tool used to remove the limbs was an ax. A bark spud was used for removing bark, which was very hard labor.

Getting to work was difficult as well. Hardee and his brother Eddie did not have a car or any other mode of transportation. Hardee, Eddie, and the other men had to walk almost twenty miles to work. After a long day of working, twenty miles was too far to walk back home in the evenings. The men had to stay in Ludowici and work Monday through Friday.

After putting in a full day of work after a long work week on Friday, the men would walk back home to Riceboro for the weekend. And before daylight on Monday morning, they would start the ritual all over again, getting up at 5:00 AM on Monday mornings and taking that long journey back to work in Ludowici.

The trail the men used to travel to work was not on any of the roads. They took a path through the woods and swamp, which was a shortcut and the shortest distance of traveling to and from Ludowici. When the men get off work on Friday evenings, the sun was setting and the dark of night began to set in. They had to carry fire torches through the path to find their way through the dark woods and swamps at night.

My grandmother Sissy told us about this incident that happened one Friday evening while the men were walking back home. "One night, my daddy, Hardee, and the other men were walking back from work from Ludowici through the woods. It was late Friday evening and just getting dark. So they had to use a torch to find their way through the dark, swampy woods. Then all of a sudden, they heard some noises in the woods. It was a loud cry of a mountain lion."

Until the late 1800s, mountain lions, also known as cougars or panthers, were common throughout the southeastern United States. Over the years, the big-cats became prey as settlers targeted them for their fur and hunted them to protect their livestock. That was one of the reasons the big-cat populations diminished.

Sissy continued by saying, "The men didn't know from what direction the big-cat sounds were coming from. They were so scared! My daddy started swinging the torch side to side trying to scare that big-cat away. Suddenly the cry got closer to them. As my daddy kept swinging that torch from side to side and twirling it around and over his head, the flame was getting smaller, because he was swinging it too fast and putting the torch out. The flame was almost out, and he stopped twirling the torch. The mountain lion was about to leap on him when the torch caught the air and burst back into flame. The flame startled the mountain lion and scared it away. The men looked at each other and said, 'Boys, we need to get out of these here woods!' Those men ran as fast as they could through that dark swamp, like runaway slaves running for their freedom." After telling that story, Sissy would laugh out loud and say, "They were lucky that night."

After a long week of cut-dying, Hardee still had to perform his household chores on the weekend. There was no rest. On Saturdays, he had to tend to his crops and plow the fields with his mule, as his wife, Rosa, worked beside him in the field. Sissy would tell us how her mother, Rosa, would carry baskets on her head while working in the field. "My mother could balance a basket of vegetables on her head real good, even while walking and bending down to pick the vegetables in the fields." On Sundays the King family would go to church as a unit. These are some of the sacrifices a family man such as Hardee had to endure to provide for his family.

Essentially, he worked six days a week with one day of rest with the family. Hardee was buried at Varnadoe Cemetery in Riceboro, Georgia, in 1944.

Hardee King and Rosa (Quarterman) King had eight children. There were five sons and three daughters. All were born and raised on South Hampton Island. Later, they moved to the Chapman community in the mid-1920s. The names of their children were Peter King, Jessie King, Annie King, Ernest King, Everlena King, Henry King, Robert "Robbie" King, and Lula King. The names were given to me by Annie (King) Wilkins.

Peter King was the oldest child born to Hardee. Peter was an entrepreneur who owned a store off Highway US 17 in Riceboro. The store was much larger than his uncle Eddie King's store. Peter married an African-American woman from Jacksonville, Florida, named Pearl F. Together they had no children. Peter King was buried at First Zion Baptist Church Cemetery in Riceboro.

Jessie King was born on South Hampton Island. He was the first child born to Hardee and Rosa. Jessie worked as a logger in Liberty County, in the mid-1930s. One day, he had an accident working in the woods cutting a log. The log came down and broke his leg. The other loggers placed a splint on his leg. Unfortunately, the broken bone in the leg was not aligned properly in the splint, which caused a permanent deformity. His leg remained crooked for the rest of his life. Jessie was married to an African-American woman named Frances Roberts from Riceboro. Jessie and Frances were separated during the period of their marriage. While they were estranged and living apart, Jessie met Willie Mae Gargin from Jacksonville, Florida. They lived together and had one daughter together in 1939. Some years later, Jessie and his estranged wife Frances got back together and moved to Brooklyn, New York in the 1940s to start a life.

Following in the footsteps of the King family, Jessie became an entrepreneur in Brooklyn and owned a store. He also owned a building near Utica Avenue and Pacific Street. His daughter in Florida never received any entitlement from his businesses, properties, or money when he died. Jessie was buried in Brooklyn in the late 1970s.

My grandmother Annie "Sissy" King was born on South Hampton Island. She was the second child born to Hardee and Rosa. Sissy was born on September 23, 1911, just six days after the death of her grandfather Roswell King III. Roswell III died on September 17, 1911, never capturing the life and virtue of his newborn granddaughter, Annie.

Annie (King) Wilkins photograph at home. She is the daughter of Hardee King and the granddaughter of Roswell King III and Mariah Guerard.

While Annie was growing up, she looked at everything so humbly and honestly. The nickname Sissy was a childhood name that was given to her by her siblings while she was just a little girl living on South Hampton Island. Sissy was educated in the Liberty County School System. The schoolhouse was in an old church house in the Retreat community of Riceboro, Georgia. She had to walk more than two miles to school from their home on South Hampton Island to the Retreat community. She was also homeschooled by her grandmother Mariah.

Annie married Josh Wilkins of Riceboro in 1932. When Josh married Annie, his family members and friends saw that Annie's skin tone was fair-skinned. They said, "Josh done gone and married a white umman." Umman is a Gullah Geechee word for woman.

Josh later became a deacon at First African Baptist Church in Riceboro, Georgia. Together they had five children. Sissy's early profession was washing and ironing clothes for people, and she was later employed at SeaPak Seafood Factory as a packer. Later she was a domestic engineer rearing her children and grandchildren while imparting knowledge and wisdom and sharing her heritage. Sissy was a member of First Zion Baptist Church. She was baptized at an early age at the Historic Baptismal Trail in Riceboro, Georgia, as well as several of her siblings. She served as a faithful member and the mother of the church. Sissy was buried at First African Baptist Church in Riceboro, Georgia, in 1990.

Ernest King was born on South Hampton Island. He was the third child born to Hardee and Rosa. Ernest's professions were carpentry and logging. Later, he worked as a janitor at the Liberty County Elementary School until he retired. Ernest married Nancy West, and they had one daughter. After Nancy died, he later married Rosella West. They had no children. Ernest King was buried at Varnadoe Cemetery in Riceboro.

Everlena King was born on South Hampton Island. She was the fourth child born to Hardee and Rosa. Everlena took after her mother, Rosa. She was a great help to her mother in becoming a great homemaker. Everlena married Randolph Roberts. Together they had two children. Everlena was a dedicated wife and mother. Her mother was very instrumental in helping her raise the children. Everlena (King) Roberts was buried at Varnadoe Cemetery in Riceboro.

Henry King was born on South Hampton Island. He was the fifth child born to Hardee and Rosa. He died at nine years old. Henry was very sick as a little boy. He had an illness that caused blood in his urine when he urinated. It may have been a bladder or kidney infection, or it may have been an early warning sign of kidney, urethral, or bladder cancer. Nonetheless, Henry hid his symptom from his mother and father, Rosa and Hardee.

When his mother finally found out about his bloody urinary tract infection, she took him to the doctor, but it was too late. It was determined by the doctor that Henry had hematuria. The infection had destroyed Henry's kidneys. Henry died the next day. Comparatively, his brother Robert "Robbie" King got the same illness, but he told his mother, Mariah, right away about his symptoms. She took him to the doctor in Ludowici,

Georgia, the following day. Happily, the doctor treated and cured Robert's illness with medication, saving his life. Henry King was buried at South Hampton Island Cemetery in Liberty County during the time the King family lived on South Hampton Island.

Robert "Robbie" King was born on South Hampton Island. He was the sixth child born to Hardee and Rosa. He first was employed as a gardener-landscaper until he entered the United States Army during World War II. He served in the military from 1942 to 1946. After his military tour, he moved to Miami and resumed his former trade as a self-employed gardener-landscaper until his retirement in 1991. Robert was married to a woman from the Bahamas named Rita. They had no children in this union, but he had one daughter with a different woman. Robert King was buried in Miami, Florida, in 1996.

Robert "Robbie" King, and Frances "Babe" (King) Caple sitting together on the porch at the Midway Museum, in Midway, Liberty County, Georgia. Robbie is the son of Hardee King and the grandson of Roswell King III and Mariah Guerard. Babe is the daughter of Rosa King and the granddaughter of Roswell King III and Mariah Guerard.

Lula King was born on South Hampton Island. She was the youngest child born of Hardee and Rosa. She was never married but had one child who survived. She died at the young age of eighteen from complications from her second pregnancy, in which she and the baby died. Lula King was buried at Varnadoe Cemetery in Riceboro, Georgia.

Lula King is standing with two friends. Lula is on the left. She is the daughter of Hardee King and the granddaughter of Roswell King III and Mariah Guerard.

Eddie King was born on South Hampton Island. He was the second of six children born to Roswell King III and Mariah Guerard. Eddie never married and had no children. He was an entrepreneur who owned a store on Ladson Road in the 1930s. (Ladson Road is now called Peter King Road.) It was one of the first businesses owned by a person of non-white descent in the city of Riceboro. Eddie King was buried at Varnadoe Cemetery in Riceboro.

Mariah King was born on South Hampton Island. She was the fifth of six children born to Roswell King III and Mariah Guerard. Mariah was named after her mother. Mariah King married an African-American man named Edward Cook. They had no children. Edward was the brother of her sister Eva's first husband, Robert Cook. Mariah (King) Cook was also buried at Varnadoe Cemetery in Riceboro.

Rosa King was born on South Hampton Island. She was the third of six children born to Roswell King III and Mariah Guerard. Rosa had the same name as her brother Hardee's wife. Rosa King was never married but had three children with African-American men. She had two daughters and one son. Rosa's professional skill was being a hairstylist. She managed a salon and styled clients with different hair textures from fine to coarse. She also managed and styled the hair of her daughter and nieces. Rosa taught the profession of hairstyling to her daughters.

Rosa King portrait. She is the daughter of Roswell King III and Mariah Guerard.

Eva King was born on June 11, 1894, on South Hampton Island. Eva was the fourth of six children born to Roswell King III and Mariah Guerard. She met and married an African-American man named Robert Cook in 1911. He preceded her in death in 1912. To this union, one child was born. Eva lived on South Hampton Island until her family was run off the land in 1924. She later met and married Lawrence Jones, who preceded her in death in 1961. In 1937 she joined the First Zion Baptist Church in Riceboro, Georgia, where she served as a faithful member and the mother of the church. She lived with her son, Roswell Cook, for two years before her death on May 20, 1978. Aunt Eva was buried at Varnadoe Cemetery in Riceboro.

Eva (King) Jones is sitting on the couch at her home. She is the daughter of Roswell King III and Mariah Guerard.

Eva (King) Jones is sitting on the couch holding a hand fan after a church revival.

Marie King was born on South Hampton Island. She was the six of six children born to Roswell King III and Mariah Guerard. She never married and had no children. Marie was sixteen years old when she died and buried in South Hampton Island Cemetery.

Marie King portrait. She is the daughter of Roswell King III and Mariah Guerard.

Marie King portrait of a side view. This is the last picture of her before she died at the age of 16 years old.

II. These are Roswell King III and Mariah Guerard's grandchildren:

Frances "Babe" King was born on South Hampton Island. She was the eldest daughter of Rosa King, and the first cousin of my grandmother Annie (King) Wilkins. Frances was a beautiful, energetic person with a bubbly personality. The first thing people noticed about Frances was her smile. She was known by her childhood nickname, Babe, by the King family.

Frances learned the profession of hairstylist from her mother. She began her career as a cosmetologist offering the latest hairstyles in New York. As time progressed, the entrepreneurial spirit in this fifth generation of Roswell King's lineage was her driving force in infiltrating the economy of New York.

After living on South Hampton Island, at the age of fifteen years old, she moved to Manhattan, New York in 1921 and fearlessly triumphed in a new culture. There she met and married her first husband, George Curtis. Frances was a vivacious and very successful business manager. She was a self-employed entrepreneur who owned several hairstyling beauty salons. She began her career as a cosmetologist offering the latest hairstyles in New York. She established a Beauty Salon in 1935 in Bronx, New York at the age of twenty nine, and was name Frances Beauty Salon. It specialized in all the latest styles, facials, hair dyeing, manicuring, and scalp treatments.

She styled hair for many famous people. One of her customers and close friends was singer, songwriter, guitarist, and recording artist Rosetta Tharpe. Sister Rosetta was mostly famous for gospel music. She is also known for jazz, blues, and rhythm and blues, as both a singer and a guitarist. As a renowned hairstylist and an entrepreneur, Frances knew many famous entertainers.

She stored her memorabilia of the rich and famous she met while living in New York. She showed me a picture in her photo album of Rosetta Tharpe. Frances would reminisce with a smile on her face and say, "Sister Rosetta—now that was my girl." Frances and her husband often saw Rosetta Tharpe perform in nightclubs in Harlem. In her photo album, she also showed a picture of heavyweight boxer Joe Lewis. The champion Joe

Lewis was also a close friend of Frances. He and others in New York City, especially Harlem, knew her by the nickname of Frankie. Frankie was the name that was given to her by her upstate friends.

Frances "Babe" (King) Caples self-photograph. She is the daughter of Rosa King and granddaughter of Roswell King III and Mariah Guerard. Frances was a self-employed entrepreneur who owned several hairstyling beauty salons in Bronx, New York

One of Frances Beauty Salon's Hair Show in Bronx, New York. Frances is standing in the doorway entrance, to the right of the picture. She specializes in all the latest styles, facials, hair dyeing, manicuring, and scalp treatments.

Frances (King) Caples took a photograph of her league cricket sports team in the 1930s. She was the first African-American woman who was a sports manager and owner of a league cricket sports team. Frances is seen standing with members of the team and coaching staff. She is seen on the left of the picture.

Frances was a very active lady. She was the first African-American woman who was a sports manager in the 1930s. She was the owner of a league cricket sports team. She also was an honorary member of the Mid Harlem Homer Club, the only local organization of pigeon fanciers in 1938.

Frances later married Willie K. Caple, who preceded her in death. In her later years, Frances became ill and her family moved her from New York back to her hometown of Riceboro, Georgia. While she was very sick and bedridden, Frances moved into the house of her nephew and his family. Her nephew and niece, which were her first cousin Annie's children, oversaw her in her last days. Frances (King, later Caple) Curtis was buried at the Varnadoe Cemetery in Riceboro in 2000.

Johnny King was born on South Hampton Island. He was the son of Rosa King and the brother of Frances. Johnny was also known as Sanka by his family. The nickname Sanka means humble. He died as a young man from drowning while swimming in the South Hampton River. The King children were very good swimmers. But one day the river current overtook Johnny, and he never came up for air. Johnny King was buried in South Hampton Island Cemetery.

Roswell King III's Second Family's Lineage

Johnny King portrait. He is the son of Rose King and grandson of Roswell King III and Mariah Guerard. This is the last picture of him before he died as a teenager from drowning.

Mamie King was born on South Hampton Island. She was the youngest daughter of Rosa King. Mamie married Ismond Jones, who was the younger brother of Lawrence Jones. Lawrence was the deceased husband of her aunt Eva King. There were no children born of this marriage. Mamie King was buried at Varnadoe Cemetery in Riceboro.

Roswell "Ross" Cook was born on South Hampton Island. He was the only child of Eva King and her first husband, Robert Cook. He was named after his grandfather Roswell III. Roswell married Estella. After the divorce, he married a second wife named Frances.

Roswell "Ross" Cook and wife Estella Roberts. He is the son of Eva (Cook) Jones and grandson of Roswell King III and Mariah Guerard.

Roswell Cook and mother Eva (King) Jones standing in their cow pasture on the 110 Acres of property in Riceboro, Georgia. This was land the King family bought after they were run off the land in 1924.

Frances's nickname was Doll. She had one son from another man before they married. Roswell and Doll took in a baby girl from Savannah, Georgia, and raised her as their own. The baby was never officially adopted by Roswell and his wife, Doll. Sissy stated, "The baby girl's father first raised her by himself after her mother died. Doll knew the man as an acquaintance. The man told Doll that he needed someone to help raise the baby. He said, 'Can you take her and raise her?' So Roswell and Doll decided to raise the baby girl. They raised the baby until she was a teenager. She was no blood relation to the King family."

Roswell Cook served as a member of the First Zion Baptist Church in Riceboro. Roswell was buried at Varnadoe Cemetery in Riceboro.

Roswell III and Mariah's children and grandchildren were either buried in the graves in the South Hampton Island Cemetery or the graves at Varnadoe Cemetery in Riceboro, except for Jessie, Robert, and Annie. The family member who died before September 1924 was buried at South Hampton Island Cemetery. That was the year the King family members were run off the Island and forbidden to return.

Some of the King family graves at both cemeteries have unmarked graves and no tombstones. I asked Sissy while she was still alive, "Why are some of these gravesites unmarked and some have no tombstones?" She said, "Times were rough back in those days. And people had very little money. They simply couldn't afford a headstone or a tombstone. In some of the older graves in the 1800s and early 1900s, people were buried in wooden coffins or boxes. And others, their bodies were wrapped and just put in the ground to be buried. They did not have the money to afford real caskets."

According to the 1910 United States Federal Census in the Militia District 15 of Liberty County, Georgia, Roswell III, Mariah, and their six children lived in one household on South Hampton Island.[16] The language the mulatto King family spoke was a combination of two types: a deep southern dialect that they inherited from their Caucasian family and the Gullah Geechee language that they inherited from the African-American population living in coastal Georgia.

When the 1910 census recorder came to South Hampton Island and asked the mulatto Kings their last names, they said their last name was King (K-I-N-G). But with their deep southern dialect and Gullah Geechees accent, it sounded like they said Karg. As a result, the census recorder spelled their last name K-A-R-G. Today you can still hear that speech pattern in coastal Georgia, which is a distinctive pronunciation of the vowel in some words such as *arg* or *ang* that should be pronounced as *ing*. Other words they used were *duh* for *the*, *da* for *they*, *gwine* for *going*, *chern* or *chillen* for *children*, and *yuh* for *here*.

On New Year's Day of 1911, while the King family was living in South Hampton Island, two of Mariah's daughters—seventeen-year-old Eva King and her sister Marie King—decided to send their seventy-nine-year-old uncle George Frederick King a gift basket by mail for the holidays. George Frederick King was the brother of Roswell III. He was better known by his middle name Frederick or just Fred.

Overwhelmed with love and compassion, Uncle Frederick replied with a letter on January 9, 1911, expressing his gratitude for the care package of food sent from his nieces Eva and Marie. He thanked them for their kind gifts of oranges, cake, and chicken.

In the letter, Uncle Frederick referred to his nieces as "My dear children." He called them children because he knew Eva and Marie were related to him and were the daughters of his younger brother Roswell III. Uncle George Frederick "Fred" King signed the letter, "Yours truly, G F King."

III. The content of the two-page letter from Frederick reads:

My dear Children,

I call you children. Don't get hot. I suppose you call yourselves grown folks, and so you are. But to an old blade who feels as if he was 110 years old, most everyone is young, even some Grand Daddy. Bo-Peeps letter received. Thanks for it. The New Year's gift also received. Many, Many thanks for it, and for the kind feeling for a poor lonely old man; Oranges fine, Cake out of sight, Chicken jam up. The cold weather just suites the cooked chicken, it would have been hard to satisfy with such good company, cake, and oranges. It was highly appreciated, and I again thank you for the gift. I wish I was with you all. I am smelling the patches here in this neck of the woods. . . . In the spring, he describe how everybody put fire out in the range. They caused the wood to burn the old wiregrass for the cattle to get fresh grass, some scrubs. If he had one goat, will turn the fire loose, it is to be ready for these fires that has swamped me. A renter, two plow man, a fruitful vine, 14 children, himself and wife, 16 all total. Pulls out, without two weeks notice. He owed me nothing, rent paid, pulls out. See what a whole 16 people made, so I had to take my rations, hoe and plow to make this gap secure, me in the lead. Well I have the whole place secure, as it can well be. Did you ever feel as if you were broken in two? That is me, right now. Oh! Well. Perhaps it may get well, I hope so. Poor old Frity is on his last legs, still holding on, but it cannot be for long. His last outing is nearby. He went out with me today and could hardly get back. No one in the house, the 16 moved out, too late in the morning time to expect anyone.

Frederick lived in a rural area near a creek in Resetter, in Baker County, Georgia. He remained living in the area since the time of his tannery business in 1854, and during the time his brother Roswell III came to work with him.

The letter was mailed from R.F.D #1. The R.F.D. stood for Rural Free Delivery. It was a service provided in the United States in the early 1890s by which mail was delivered free directly to a rural farm family. Before the R.F.D. service, a person would have to pick up their mail themselves at a distant post office or pay to have it delivered.

Frederick explained how they burned the wiregrass and scrubs so that in the spring it would cause fresh grass to grow for the cattle. He furthermore commented on the hard times, and how his renters pulled out and left him without two weeks' notice. The burden it caused him made him feel as if he were broken in two. He felt stressed, emotionally drained, and mentally exhausted living as a poor, lonely old man with no family members around.

Eva kept the letter written by her uncle Frederick for many years. After Eva died in 1978, the letter was passed down to Eva's grandnephew and remained in the family's possession. Eva would mention that James Audley King and Frederick King were her favorite uncles.

Roswell III was still alive in 1911 when the letter was written to his brother Frederick. Family meant the world to Roswell III. He raised his children properly in the value of putting God first, family second, and themselves last. Roswell III loved his second family deeply and wanted to give Mariah and their children all he had to offer. By showing his love and devotion to his family, Roswell provided them with a loving home at Roswell King's South Hampton Plantation, a sense of security and, most of all, an essential lifestyle.

IV. The King's life after the move from South Hampton Island:

The Hampton Islands in coastal Georgia were divided into two halves. The Hampton River separates the North and South Hampton tracts. Behind Roswell III's house on South Hampton Island was the Hampton River. The river flowed from the Atlantic Ocean, which made it salty. Roswell III used the salty river for the production of salt. The primary method he used to extract salt from the seawater was drying it out by exposure to the sun.

Nowadays, the Hampton Island tract is embellished as a transcendent masterpiece, with a mixture of maritime forest, marshland, lakes, winding roads, miles of fathomless rivers, and tidal saltwater marshes leading to the Atlantic Ocean. Currently Hampton Island is a beautiful preservation of luxurious homes and private retreats full of breathtaking amenities. This coastal paradise of southeast Georgia is an ideal place for excitement, relaxation, and recreation that includes a golf course, riding trails, speed boats and sailboats, seaplanes, an airport, freshwater fishing, and hunting, along with rich soil to farm organic fruits and vegetables. This wonder of the world has often captivated the audience and imagination of the rich and famous. Swimming, fishing, shrimping, crabbing, and boating are popular on this remote island that transports vacationers out of a world of hustle and bustle into the epitome of heaven-on-earth ecstasy.

But in the early 1900s, especially in the deep south, lack of job opportunities impeded many lives and caused poverty. Many African-Americans migrated north to find jobs for a better way of life. This included Roswell III's son Jessie King and his granddaughter Frances "Babe" (King) Caple.

The 1940s proved to be a time of economic destitution. The death of Mariah Guerard, a major matriarch of the King family, and the death of Hardee King, also known as Papa Hardee or just Papa, made life very difficult for Rosa and her daughters. Rosa (Quarterman) King was also known by her family as Momma Rosa or just Momma. Momma Rosa, Everlena King, and her sixteen-year-old daughter, Lula King, were left to live in the home alone after the aforementioned's passing.

Momma Rosa was too old to work. Everlena, her two sons, and Lula were barely making a decent living. Jobs were scarce. The only jobs available in Riceboro were laundry service, timber, planting, and sharecropping. To find employment, one would have to travel as far as Savannah, Georgia, or sometimes travel to South Carolina, which was even further. By having no jobs, they had to rely on government assistance for aid. The national welfare system was established in 1935. They received only sixteen dollars a month from welfare.

In 1945 Lula King became pregnant at the age of sixteen. Times were hard when having a baby without a husband. She had nothing—no money to raise the baby after he was born. In October Lula had a complication during her pregnancy and gave birth during her third trimester, in the seventh month. The premature baby boy weighed just two pounds when he was born. The doctors at the Jesup, Georgia, hospital kept the baby in the hospital for almost two months, until he was strong enough to go home. Brother Peter King would drive Lula and her sister Annie "Sissy" to check on the baby while he was in the hospital.

In December, the hospital wrote Lula and Sissy a letter that said it was time to get the baby; he was healthy enough to go home. Back in those days, no one had a telephone in their home, so writing a letter was the only way the hospital could get a message to the mother.

When it was time for the baby to come home from the hospital, Lula asked Sissy to get the baby. The next day, Sissy's husband, Josh, made arrangements with Mr. Hargrove to drive her to the hospital. On a cold day in December, they went to pick up the tiny premature baby. Sissy wore a winter coat on that day and did not bring a blanket. She thought the hospital would provide with one, but the hospital did not. So she had to wrap the tiny baby in her coat to keep him warm for the journey home.

Mr. Hargrove drove Sissy back to Riceboro. She asked Mr. Hargrove to drop her and the baby off at the Cross Road community near the Cross Road school. Once at Cross Road, she asked the bus driver if she could catch a ride home along with the school kids.

Sissy got on the bus with the baby swaddled in her coat. No one on the school bus knew Sissy had a baby wrapped in her coat. When she got home, she called her children together and said to them, "Here is your new brother. This is Lula's baby. We are going to raise him." The children were so happy about the new addition to the family.

After bringing the baby to Lula, Lula said to her sister, "Sissy, you have a home, and your husband, Josh, is working. You can take care of the baby better than me. I want my baby, but I would rather you would have him. I cannot provide for him. I don't have anything. My Momma Rosa doesn't have anything. I can't even buy milk for him. I don't have a job."

At that time, Lula was living with her mother, Rosa (Quarterman) King. Rosa was a widow, as her husband, Hardee King, had died a year earlier in 1944. She was barely making a living of her own. Having an extra mouth to feed, and with no husband, life was difficult.

Sissy said to Lula, "This is your only child. If ever you want him, you can come and get him at anytime." The baby boy was name Melvin King.

Lula called Sissy by her given name, Annie, and said, "No, Annie. If you raise him, you can keep him. I will never take him back from you. Anytime you need me to come down and help with the baby, I will be there to help out." One time the baby was very sick, and Sissy called Lula to help with him. Lula came and stayed with Sissy and Josh until the baby was well. She stayed with her sister often to help out with the baby from time to time.

When the baby became one year old, Lula left Riceboro, Georgia, and moved to Miami, Florida, to find a job. She was hoping to find work and get a new start in life and be able to better provide for herself and her baby.

Lula worked in Miami, where she became pregnant again with her second baby. Lula had complications in her pregnancy during her last trimester, as with her first baby. However, the baby died inside her womb. She did not know she had a stillborn. She became very ill. Lula died due to complications with the pregnancy. Her body was transported back to Riceboro, Georgia, where she was buried at Varnadoe Cemetery, along with her baby.

Lula's mother, Momma Rosa, blamed herself for Lula's death. She felt responsible because she had allowed her seventeen-year-old daughter to go off with a man she had never seen before. Momma Rosa would cry and say, "That man must have put root on me, because I would have never let my child go off with a man I had never seen before." When Lula said the man was coming to get her, she had said to Lula, "You will never go with him." But when the man came, her mind changed as quickly as that. She told Lula she could go. "You know that ain't me. I wouldn't let my daughter go with a man I don't know anything 'bout. I don't know why." If she had said no, then Lula would not have left. Momma Rosa took that guilt to her grave.

After the death of Lula, Momma Rosa, Everlena, and her two sons continued to live in the house in the Chapman community. They lived in a three-room house with no running water, no electricity, and an outhouse.

With the little money they were receiving from government assistance, some money was used to buy food, such as rice. They would buy a twenty-five-pound sack of rice for their meals. When the rice sacks were empty, the

King women would use the sacks to make beautiful clothing for the family. It may seem like they had little, but with what they had, they managed to use their resources wisely.

The King family was sustained by growing their food. Before his death, Hardee harvested many fruit trees, such as apples, figs, persimmons, peaches, pears, and dates, as well as pecan trees and a huge white grape orchard just walking distance from the house.

The King family did not need money to buy vegetables, since planting was not a foreign concept. They were good planters. Even the children helped with planting and harvesting beans, peas, potatoes, corn, tomatoes, greens, and watermelons. The vegetables were placed in jars for preservation, which kept them fresh for months at a time. They also didn't need money to buy meat, since they supplied their own source of meat from fishing and their livestock. The cows supplied their need for milk and butter.

Sissy and her husband, Josh, were essential to the needs of Momma Rosa and her household. They also had a hand in making sure Momma Rosa was taken care of. Josh was the man of the land. He was a skilled planter. From his crop harvest, he also shared with his mother-in-law's household and supplied the family with vegetables from his fields. He also was an experienced hunter and a first-rate fisherman.

Josh raised his hogs, and he also shared meat from the hogs with the rest of the King family. The meats were kept in a smokehouse. A smokehouse is a building in which meat is cured with smoke for preservation. Meat from the slaughter of hogs was salted and hung up in the dark smoke-filled room to preserve it for weeks or even months.

Before the late 1940s, the King family did not have a refrigerator or freezer, so the smokehouse had to be used to best keep the meats cured. So sixteen dollars a month for government assistance goes a long way when you have other means of survival and with the help of loved ones.

Chapter 4

The Land at Roswell King's South Hampton Plantation

Roswell King III, Mariah Guerard, and their children and grandchildren lived on a 1,960-acre tract of land at South Hampton Plantation. Roswell III lived on South Hampton Plantation until his death on September 17, 1911, at the age of seventy-five. Mariah and her family continued to live on the land until they were run off in September 1924.

South Hampton Plantation has been mentioned many times in this book and can be identified under three different names: Roswell King's South Hampton Plantation, South Hampton Island, and South Hampton Preserve. These 1,960 acres of land were once bought by Roswell King Jr. in 1838. Later the land was willed to his wife, Julia Rebecca Maxwell King. A piece of land that measures 1,960 acres is equivalent of 3.0625 square miles, or 7.931839 square kilometers.

According to Certificate of Title Search 2006, under a certain trust deed dated April 1, 1880, between Mrs. Julia and her son Roswell III, he subsequently acquired the 1,960 acres of land known as Roswell King's South Hampton Plantation in Liberty County, Georgia. And with this agreement, Roswell III became the new trustee of Roswell King's South Hampton Plantation.[17]

The members of the King family desperately wanted to get the tract of land from Roswell III. They had a vendetta against Roswell III because of his second family. The King family learned that Roswell III wrote a will before he died, leaving all his worldly possessions—a living trust, money, estates, and properties (including his tract of land at South Hampton Plantation)—to his second family in coastal Georgia.

Instead of having Roswell III's inheritance pass down to Mariah and her children when he died, they kept his will out of probate to prevent Mariah from finding out. Was this a conspiracy to commit fraud? Had Roswell III known about the scheme, he almost certainly would have stopped it from happening. His siblings and other relatives came together in 1908 to plot to take Roswell King's South Hampton Plantation from him.

In 2006 the family descendants of Roswell III, who are the members of his second family of coastal Georgia, decided to have a title search of public records perform for the King family in Liberty County, Georgia. These court house records revealed some shocking truths about quick claim deeds, last will and testaments, and notarized documents that took place during the late nineteenth and early twentieth centuries by the King family members.

Roswell King Jr., the father of Roswell III, wrote a last will and testament, but it was not dated until April 1880, twenty-six years after his death, as Roswell Jr. died in 1854. His nephew Reverend Charles B. King was the administrator of his will. Reverend Charles was the son of Barrington King Sr. And Barrington Sr. was the brother of Roswell Jr. In his will, under his fifth wish, Roswell Jr. stated if his wife Julia be so imprudent as to marry again, that her husband have no control over the property or children. However, Mrs. Julia's individual property would be used at her disposal.

To ensure her husband's property remained in the King family's control, Mrs. Julia made her favorite son, Roswell III, trustee of the South Hampton Plantation. Roswell III was the best choice during 1880 to be the trustee of his father's South Hampton Plantation. At the time, he was not married, since his wife, Catherine had died in 1872. With him not being married, the land could remain with one of Roswell King Jr.'s children with no reprisal. The land was conveyed to Roswell III before he started a second family with his housemaid, Mariah Guerard. Roswell III and Mariah's second family began in 1884 with the birth of their first child, Hardee King.

Eventually Roswell III and Mariah had six children together. They were considered Roswell III's second family. Even though Roswell III had six children from his previous wife, he was determined to make his second family his heirs. This angered the other King family members. Because Roswell III was his mother's favorite, the other King's family members did not dare to cross him while his mother was still alive. His mother, Mrs. Julia, later died in 1892.

A conspiracy arose in 1908 that took place sixteen years after the death of Mrs. Julia and twenty-eight years after the release of Roswell Jr.'s will. A group of Roswell III's siblings and other relatives came together to plot and falsify claims to try to steal Roswell King's South Hampton Plantation away from him. In fact, several transactions occurred against him by his family members.

One notarized document took place in June 1908, but was not recorded until December 12, 1908, in Pensacola, Florida. Apparently, this notarized document claimed that Roswell III did a quick claim deed of the tract of land and granted it to his sister-in-law, Elizabeth Catherine King, and his children from his first wife. Elizabeth Catherine was married to Roswell III's brother, James Audley Maxwell King. Elizabeth Catherine and James Audley were the ones who took in and raised Roswell III's children after his wife, Catherine died. The document claimed that Roswell III did a quick claim of the land, meaning the 1,960 acres known as Roswell King's South Hampton Plantation, and granted it to his sister-in-law, Elizabeth Catherine, and children. And the notarized document was supposedly signed by Roswell B. King IV. Roswell IV was Roswell King III's second-oldest son from his first family. "This document should not have been valid, because the land was willed to his father, Roswell III."[18]

I have read this agreement in its entirety, and it brought to my attention a very apprehensive question concerning the validity of this document. The question is, why would Roswell B. King IV grant a quick claim deed of the 1,960 acres of land to his aunt Elizabeth Catherine and the children? Certainly, this was Elizabeth Catherine and her nephew Roswell IV's attempt to steal the land from his father. Roswell III was currently living on South Hampton Plantation along with Mariah Guerard, their children, and their grandchildren during 1908. Roswell III was seventy-two years old at the time his sister-in-law, son, and family members tried to steal the land from him.

Yet another suspicious action by a notarized document took place in June 1908 in Savannah, Georgia. Elizabeth Catherine did another quick claim deed with Robert Roswell King. Robert was her nephew and the son of John Butler King and Mary Agnes Battey King. John was the brother of Roswell III. As a matter of fact, in June 1908, there were several other quick claim deeds done between other King family members concerning the land at South Hampton Plantation. "The handwritten notarized document claimed that under oath the deed was signed in their presence by Roswell King III. In fact, Roswell III did not have any knowledge of the quick claim deeds, and he did not sign the notarized document."[19]

In the early 1900s, it was common for the county clerk's office to write and sign the signatures in the book of deeds and on other court documents. It was more legible and easier to read with just one person's handwriting. The county clerk was the official keeper of all public records for the county. The clerk's office was responsible for processing all real property transactions, plats, and deeds.

"A third notarized document was made by R. G. Tunno. He was married to Roswell III's sister Isabel Cooper King. R. G. Tunno said in the document that he witnessed Roswell King III sign the deed to the 1,960 acres of Roswell King's South Hampton Plantation, which supposedly granted the land to Elizabeth Catherine and the children."[20] Again, did Roswell III truly sign the deed in the presence of R. G. Tunno? If so, was this done intentionally or under false pretenses?

I truly believed these quick claim deeds were without merit. It seems as though the King family members manipulated the legal system to get the deed to Roswell III's land in South Hampton. A quick claim deed is a method of granting title to another person or transferring property between family members. So why would Roswell III sign over his land and property when he and his family were living on South Hampton Plantation?

The Land at Roswell King's South Hampton Plantation

Many times we have read or heard about the horrors of people taking land or property from other people, especially during the latter part of the nineteenth century and early twentieth century. If a thief takes possession of another person property, should not his possession be returned to the owner if determined the possession was stolen, or would he be compensated for the loss?

Yet a fourth conspiracy took place in 1908. A notarized document was recorded on July 13, 1908, in Chatham County, Georgia (Savannah). "Apparently ten of Roswell King III's siblings and other family members had mysteriously taken ownership of the entire estate of the 1,960 acres of Roswell King's South Hampton Plantation. This indention was made and entered on June 29, 1908, between George Frederick King of Baker County, Georgia; Roswell B. King IV of Liberty County, Georgia; Isabel C. Tunno of Chatham County, Georgia; Georgia B. King of Franklin County, Tennessee; Daisy Anderson King of Franklin County, Tennessee; Isabel Maxwell Valentine of Buncome County, North Carolina; Bayard H. King of Polk County, Florida; Mary Battey King of Floyd County, Georgia; Battey King of Fulton County, Georgia; C. B. Hendry of Liberty County, Georgia; and F. Henry of Liberty County, Georgia."[21] Together, all parties signed the quick deed claim, and together they surprisingly now owned the entire estate of the South Hampton Plantation. The family decided to sell the land. They sold the land, without the knowledge of Roswell King III, to J. R. Paschall of Warren County, North Carolina, and Thomas Gresham of Virginia, coparties under the name of Paschall and Gresham.

"Jointly, Roswell III's brother George Frederick King, along with other King family members, met together and secretly conspired and sold the deed to Roswell King's South Hampton Plantation for $10,000 to Paschall and Gresham, dated June 29, 1908. J. R. Paschall and Thomas Gresham were partners in business as a timber company. It is recorded in the clerk's office in Liberty County Superior Court, in Book of Deeds A.I. pages 484–485."[22]

"In 1924 Paschall and Gresham sold the tract of property to Sunbury Lumber Company. Since that date, the land was sold several times to different companies, including Gay Green of Asheville, North Carolina in September 1924, and Union Bags and Timber Company, later called Union Camp Corporation in 1936."[23] In 1924 was the same year Mariah Guerard, her children, and her grandchildren were run off the land at South Hampton Plantation.

The sales of the land may not have been valid. The land was bought by Roswell King Jr. in 1838. After his death, he willed the land to his wife, Julia. And under a certain trust deed, she conveyed the land to her son Roswell King III, making him the trustee of Roswell King's South Hampton Plantation.

Some people believed by October 1867, Roswell King III would not clear expenses at South Hampton because planting was not successful and he was in debt. This is a misunderstanding. His debt in 1867 was not in South Hampton. The debt that Roswell III accumulated was during the time he farmed in Walthourville. He speaks of trying it one year longer, hoping to make money enough to buy a farm outside of Liberty County. But instead, he and his family left his farm in Walthourville and took root at Roswell King's South Hampton Plantation.

The King family's fraudulent schemes seem to have worked. The land was taken from Roswell III's second family. Was it for a profit gain or another reason? Maybe both. The other reason may have been because Mariah and her children were not of the white race. They were a mixture of Native American, Jewish, Caucasian, and African-American descent. Corruption played a big part in stealing the land from Roswell King III and his true heirs.

I. Skeletal remains:

In the late 1970s, the state of Georgia was digging a soil pit on South Hampton Island in Liberty County, east of Interstate Highway 95 and south of the North Newport River and Payne Creek, for the completion of the Interstate. While digging, state employees noticed they had dug up skeletal remains behind the big oak tree. The tree is near the site where Roswell III's plantation home was once located, and where Mariah Guerard and her family were run off their land in 1924. After state employees discovered the bones, they contacted the camp ranger at Camp Blue Heron, Boy Scouts of America, to view what they had found.

Camp Blue Heron, Boy Scouts of America was also located on South Hampton Island. The camp ranger instantly contacted one of Roswell III's Black descendants who lived in Riceboro so they could go to the site to verify and identify the skeletal remains. The camp ranger visited Firman Wilkins at his residence because he knew Firman was a Black descendant of Roswell III. Firman's bloodline to the King family dates back to his mother, Annie (King) Wilkins, grandfather Hardee King, and great-grandfather Roswell King III.

Once the state of Georgia determined there were still graves on the premises, they ordered no more digging in that vicinity of South Hampton Island. So digging ceased at the gravesite. However, they were allowed to dig three hundred feet from that spot.

Firman then contacted his brother, who also lived in Riceboro. The two men immediately went to the site where the skeletons had been found. They placed rope surrounding the cemetery. Two acres were barricaded to prevent any illegal trespassers from entering the property. The gravesites remained restricted until the late 1990s until the King family members and the camp ranger re-marked the cemetery again with orange ribbons. When Aunt Eva (King) Cook was still living, she told her grandnephew Firman that some of her King ancestors were buried on South Hampton Island.

At that time, Union Camp Corporation of Savannah, Georgia—now known as International Papers—eligibly owned the 1,960 acres of land, which they had bought to harvest timber. Firman had been employed as a foreman at Union Camp since the early 1970s.

In August 2002 members of the King family attended a county commissioner's meeting in Liberty County concerning houses being built in the vicinity of the cemetery at South Hampton Island. A question that arose during the meeting was whether or not a house could be built on top of graves. The county commissioner stated that it was against the county and state laws to build houses over a cemetery or disturb a burial ground:

OCGA 44-12-260 - Protection of American Indian Human Remains and Burial Objects.

OCGA 36-72-1 - Abandoned Cemeteries and Burial Grounds.

OCGA 31-21-6 - Dead Bodies.

The Hampton Island Preserve is divided into two sections, South Hampton Island and North Hampton region, in which the Hampton River separates the two. It was once called King Causeway by the locals. The Hampton Island Preserve is approximately 4,000 acres, and the 1,960 acres of Roswell King's South Hampton Plantation are located within the Hampton Island Preserve. This preservation is an area rich with heritage, history, recreation, and miles of saltwater rivers that lead out to the Atlantic Ocean. Today this luxurious landscape features many homes that were built for the rich and famous over the years.

In 2003 a well-known celebrity wanted to purchase land located within the 1,960 acres of land on Roswell King's South Hampton Plantation. It is located east of Interstate Highway 95 and just some thirty-five miles south of Savannah, Georgia. The land originally plotted was near the South Hampton Island cemetery. Once the Liberty County commissioner found out about the land being bought by the celebrity in the vicinity of the cemetery, they stopped the plans before any soil or landscape was disturbed around the gravesite. Years later, the celebrity eventually bought an eighty-seven-acre estate on South Hampton Island and built a multimillion-dollar home in a different location. This estate is not in the vicinity of any known cemetery.

Within a week after the county commissioner meeting, a member of the Black King family and the camp ranger met with the Island Manager of Hampton Island Preserve to schedule a date to visit the general location where the skeletons had been found. The family member was unavailable

The Land at Roswell King's South Hampton Plantation

to attend at that time. So instead, the camp ranger met with the Island Manager and showed him where the skeletons were located.

After their meeting, the camp ranger called the Black King family members and stated that the Hampton Island Preserve, LLC insinuated that the cemetery was nonexistent on South Hampton Island and that it may be located on another plantation, even after the camp ranger showed him where bones were found during the completion on Interstate 95 back in the 1970s. Since the graves did not have any headstones, the Island Manager did not see any evidence of a cemetery.

The Island Manager then called the Black King family member three days later and asked how he knew the graves were on South Hampton Preserve. The family member told him that their mother, Annie "Sissy" (King) Wilkins, Aunt Eva (King) Cook, and other King relatives were born and raised on South Hampton Island. They had foreknowledge of the gravesites. Aunt Eva witnessed the burial of her father, Roswell King III, sixteen-year-old sister Marie King, nine-year-old nephew Henry King, and teenage grandnephew Johnny King, along with Native Americans who worked at South Hampton Island.

Aunt Eva stated her father, Roswell III, died on September 17, 1911, and was buried days later by his family on South Hampton Island. The event was written in the family's Bible. The graves on South Hampton Island had no headstone, but Aunt Eva remembered the locations of each of her family member's graves. She recalls that her father's grave remained on South Hampton Island even after her family was run off the land in September 1924. Sometime after 1934, a marble marker for Roswell King III was provided by the War Department and placed inside the Historical Midway Cemetery. The King family member's burial plot is located in the back section of the cemetery inside a cemented *Roswell* wall.

The Black family believes Roswell III's unmarked grave remains on South Hampton Island. And the marble marker was added as the sacred memory of the death of Roswell King III, and for serving in the Army during war time. There is no documented evident of Roswell King III or his first wife, Catherine's graves were ever excavated from South Hampton Island and moved to Midway Cemetery.

His wife, Catherine, was also buried on South Hampton Island in 1872 thirty years before her husband. The exact location of her gravesite is unknown since there is no headstone. It is thought that Catherine's body was buried near Roswell III's marble marker at the Midway Cemetery, but there is no evidence of her grave there either.

Roswell III's sister, Mary (King) Wells, died in 1871 and was also buried on South Hampton Island. There is no record of her being buried elsewhere since Georgia's statewide registration of births and deaths began in 1919 as Aunt Eva stated to the family before she died.

From November 14 through 21 2007, archival/historical research and ground-penetrating radar (GPR) investigation was conducted by request of the Hampton Island Preserve manager. The purpose of the studies was to review historical records for information to document the presence of cemeteries, family burial plots, or any gravesites on the property. The survey team consisted of two GPR survey operators, with the presence of three of the Black King family members.

The contents and results of the report are not cited in this book. However, the research omitted parts about Roswell King III's second family members and others being buried on the land and the circumstances that took place with skeletal remains during the completion of Interstate 95.

The Hampton Island Preserve bought 212 acres of Camp Blue Heron, Boys Scouts of America, for an estimated $8 million in November 2007 and gave $5 million to Coastal Empire Council, Inc., newly formed Coastal Georgia Council Boy Scouts of America, which is located within the 1,960 acres. Camp Blue Heron, Boys Scouts agreed to sell it, in part, because the development was encroaching on the camp, according to the scout executive for the Coastal Empire Council, Inc.

The Black King family felt as though the South Hampton Island, along with the Camp Blue Heron tract of land, originally belonged to Roswell King III. With the difference circumstances beginning in the early 1900s and into the 2000s, with the manipulating of the legal system and the sale of the land right from under them, they family felt betrayed. Was this the master plan employed to reject Mariah Guerard and her children as heirs to South Hampton Island?

After the Civil War, and leaving the military in 1865, Roswell III moved his family from Walthourville to Roswell King's South Hampton Plantation in 1867. In 1880, his mother made him the Trustee of Roswell King's South Hampton Plantation, and some years later, he was granted a Living Trust in Roswell, Georgia. His financial issue was of the past. The Living Trust is still active today.

Chapter 5

The Inheritance

Before the death of Roswell King III on September 17, 1911, he was completely knowledgeable of all the inheritances entitled to him as one of the heirs of the King's family. He realized his trust wealth and entitlements were very extensive. He wrote a will in the early twentieth century bequeathing his inheritance and estate to his second family in coastal Georgia. Roswell III mandated that his inheritance go as he wished. This angered the other King family members in such a way that they deliberately kept his trust from Mariah Guerard and their children.

For more than one hundred years, a copy of Roswell III's will was secretly kept and never revealed to his second family. Therefore, because of the betrayal, lies, and deception by the King family members, his second family never received anything from his will. The King family in coastal Georgia are the last of the King's heirs, who never received their inheritance.

The inheritance that Roswell III received from his King family was passed down through generations, through a series of trusts that possibly included fortunes, a living trust, properties, the land of South Hampton Plantation, shares of capital stocks, and possibly the estate of Barrington Hall, among other hidden treasures. The last known location of the will or the trust was in the city of Roswell, Georgia.

How does one put a house in a trust? The first thing you do is get a copy of your current deed. Then, you must change the title of your home from your name to the name of your trust. Then, prepare a copy of a new deed. You would need a deed form that is relevant to your state. The type of form used in

Georgia would be a quick claim deed or a grant deed. Then, fill out that form. The grantor would be your name. The grantee would be the name of the trust. Copy the legal description of the property from your current deed onto the new deed you are preparing for the trust. Sign and date it, in front of a notary, then file the record into a probate court.

A beneficiary or beneficiaries under a trust will depend on the actual language used in the trust documents to determine who receives the trust, or how it is divided. However, Roswell III's second family never obtained a copy, so they do not know exactly what is in the trust. Nevertheless, the will must be found to determine the actual details, specifically stated for the beneficiaries.

The King family's lives date back to Georgia's colonial history. The legacy of Roswell King Sr., the founder of Roswell, Georgia, started in the marshland and rivers of coastal Georgia as a justice of the peace, bank owner, slave manager, rice planter, and plantation manager. And in northern Georgia, Roswell Sr. and his son, Barrington King Sr., the co-founder of the city of Roswell, were entrepreneurs. With their fame and wealth, they were able to leave an inheritance for the King family. All their descendants reaped the benefit of their hard work.

The historical Barrington Hall in the city of Roswell, Georgia, was built by Barrington King Sr. and completed in 1842. The house remained in the King family until it was unscrupulously sold in 2003. "The probate files on Barrington King Sr. are found in Cobb County. However, he died intestate, and no wills were ever filed in the courts. Without a copy of the will, it is unclear who is the true owner of the Barrington Hall estate and property. The estate and property were believed to have been placed in a Roswell King III Trust."[24]

Barrington King Sr. lived in Barrington Hall until he died in 1866. His widow, Catherine Margaret (Nephew) King, continued to live at Barrington Hall. In 1883 Mrs. Catherine invited her daughter Evelyn "Eva" (King) Baker, her children, and her husband, Reverend William Baker, to move in with her. The Bakers then moved into Barrington Hall. Catherine Margaret King died in 1887, and the Bakers lived the remainder of their lives there. After the death of Mrs. Evelyn Baker in 1924, her grandchild Evelyn Simpson became the caretaker of Barrington Hall.

Evelyn Simpson was never willed to the Barrington Hall house. The house is believed to be willed to Barrington King Sr.'s grandnephew Roswell King III. Since Roswell III was not married, Barrington Hall can remain with one of the King's male blood relatives with no reprisal. And there would be no threat of losing the house through a divorce settlement since he was not married.

"In the early years, siblings Evelyn and Katherine "Tippy" B. Simpson lived at Barrington Hall. In 1932 it is believed that Evelyn and Katherine owned the property. But there is no evidence of Barrington King Sr. leaving the property to either of them in a will or a trust. Evelyn lived at Barrington Hall until she died in 1960 leaving a will. And in her third desire, she directs that all property of any kind go to her sister Katherine."[25] Miss Katherine continued to live alone in the home and became the new caretaker of Barrington Hall Estate. In the 1970s she met a vibrant woman named Lois Carson. Although Miss Lois had no blood relations with the King family, Miss Katherine and Miss Lois became close friends.

In 1975 Miss Katherine invited Miss Lois to move into Barrington Hall. Two years later, Miss Katherine formally adopted the fifty-seven-year-old Miss Lois on May 25, 1977. "Miss Lois changed her name from Lois Carson to Lois Virginia King Simpson."[26] Many historians believe she took advantage of Miss Katherine as she climbed the ranks of being a senior citizen. Some King family members further believed Miss Lois received some good legal advice. And because Miss Katherine was ill and in her eighties, she was easier to exploit.

Miss Lois then had Miss Katherine draft a will leaving Barrington Hall to her. Since her name then had the King's name in it, I am sure that the adoption was a ruse to defeat any attempts to caveat the will.

Miss Katherine's neighbors stated Miss Lois had come to them with a document needing the signature of a witness, and when they asked to see what they were signing, they were told, "Never mind." Suspiciously, the signature was obtained because Miss Katherine's will was changed, leaving the property to Miss Lois. Miss Lois felt if the will was found to be invalid due to undue influence or lack of capacity, then a probate court would have held that Miss Katherine died intestate and her adopted daughter, Miss Lois, would inherit through the Georgia intestacy laws. The only good thing about Miss Lois is it looks like she originally really did not have any desire to profit from this affair by selling the house.

On June 7, 1990, ABC-TV broadcast a special titled *Mansion's Authenticity Makes "Perfect Tribute" as Civil War Movie Set*, which included an exposé on Barrington Hall with Miss Lois Simpson. A month later, on July 6, 1990, Miss Katherine (grantor) signed a deed of gift to Lois (grantee) for ploys on the Barrington Hall property. The executor's deed to grant was recorded in Deed Book 5210 on page 405 in the Fulton County, Georgia, estate records. At some point after that action, page 405 in the Deed Book in Fulton County went missing from the estate records.[27]

Did someone remove page 405 from the Deed Book from the clerk's office? When was the page removed, who removed it, and for what purpose? Was the person or persons trying to keep the public from finding out something that they did not want the public to know?

There were other findings discovered during a certificate of title and public records search in August 2003 in Fulton County, Georgia. There were a series of quick deed claims and deeds of gift that were related to the transaction of Barrington Hall over the years between Katherine Baker Simpson and others.

There was a deed of gift in July 1990 from Katherine B. Simpson and Lois Virginia King Simpson to her lawyer. Another was from the lawyer of Katherine Baker Simpson. A third was from Katherine Baker Simpson to Lois Virginia Simpson. A fourth was from Lois Virginia Simpson to a financial banker as a deed of gift.[28]

The lawyer and financial banker aided Katherine Baker Simpson and Lois Virginia King Simpson with the transaction of the deed for Barrington Hall. These were some of the ways the trustee of Barrington Hall was granted from one party to the second party. Miss Katherine passed away on February 28, 1995, at the age of ninety-nine years old. After that, Miss Lois became the new caretaker of Barrington Hall. They were never heirs to the Barrington Hall Estate.

The Inheritance

I. Seems to be a pattern:

Meanwhile, an unrelated incident took place in coastal Georgia during the 1990s concerning the granddaughter of Roswell III and Mariah Guerard. Frances "Babe" (King) Caple lived in New York from the 1930s to the 1990s. She once was a very successful businesswoman, owning hair-styling beauty salons, night club, and properties in the big city. During the time she lived in New York, she would visit her family in coastal Georgia. She would either stay with her first cousin Annie (King) Wilkins, her niece, or her nephew in Riceboro during her visits.

After the death of Annie in 1990, Frances became the oldest living descendant of Roswell King III and Mariah Guerard. Therefore, she became the intestate succession of the ten acres of land that were once deeded to her late uncle Hardee King. Frances decided to divide the ten acres between her niece and nephews, who were Annie's children. Before Frances died, she told her niece and nephews, "I want all of my money and properties to go to Annie's children when I die." Frances made that claim because Annie's children were the closest family members to her. They helped her during her elder years, and while she was sick, and shut in.

Frances became ill and was hospitalized in New York. While she was in the hospital, she had an injury. Under the care of the hospital and nurses, she fell out of the hospital bed and broke her hip. Her family in Riceboro, was notified of the accident, so her nephews from Riceboro came to New York to check on her in the hospital. With the consent of Frances, her nephews obtained a lawyer in New York and took out a class-action lawsuit for negligence against the hospital. The nephews checked Frances out of the hospital and moved her to Riceboro. They also came back to New York to get all of her household belongings upon her request. While they were back in Riceboro, the family would routinely call to check with the lawyer on the progress of the lawsuit.

The lawsuit went on for months, and the nephews called the lawyer constantly to follow up on the case. The lawyer kept telling them, "The case is still being worked on. I will keep you informed." Somehow the cunningness of the big-city lawyers took advantage of the small-town nephews. The lawyer never got back in touch with the family, and Frances's family in Riceboro did not get a dime from the lawsuit. She lived at her nephew Firman's house until her death.

Another incident happened in the 1990s concerning Mariah Guerard's niece. Her name was Georgia. Georgia was born in Bluffton, South Carolina, and later in life moved to Savannah, Georgia. The niece, Georgia, had land to sell in South Carolina. She said to her cousin Firman, "Firman, I have some land I want you to sell for me. When you do, I will give you some of the proceeds from the sale of the land." Georgia wanted half of the profit from the sale of the land to go to her family in Riceboro. And she made that claim because Annie's children were the closest family member to her and always helped her and were there for her in her time of need. Georgia was not related to the King family by blood; She was related to the Guerard family.

Georgia told her plans to sell the land to a nonfamily member. This woman was raised by one of Georgia's cousins, Roswell Cook. She was no blood relation to the King or Guerard side of the family. But Roswell Cook and his wife, Doll, raised her from a baby until she was grown.

After learning Georgia's plan, somehow she, along with her pastor, convinced Georgia that they would sell the land for her. Together the woman and the pastor sold the land without the knowledge of Georgia's cousin Firman. The woman and the pastor got a lawyer and got a power of attorney to sell Georgia's land. Georgia was very sickly when this happened.

The two sold the land and kept the money from the purchase. And since the woman had power of attorney, she also had access to Georgia's bank account. And when Georgia died, she also took all of the money from the bank account. Sissy's children never received any entitlement from their cousin's land sale.

There seems to be a pattern. The descendants of Roswell King III's second family had land, money, properties, and inheritance taken away from them. This dates back from the early 1900s and spanned into the 2000s, more than one hundred years of betrayal and deceit against the King's family members.

II. Looking for the second family:

In February 2001 a member of the King family from northern Georgia came to Riceboro looking for the second family's descendants of Roswell III. The family member, whose name will remain anonymous, wanted to meet his Black kinfolks from coastal Georgia. He arrived at the Chapman community of Riceboro and met a woman who claimed to be related to the second family member of Roswell III. She told him, "I am in the King family." Actually, she was no blood relative to the King's family, but she was related to the King by marriage. She was telling the truth, from a certain point of view. Miss West was the sister of Rosella (West) King. Mrs. Rosella was married to the late Ernest King. Ernest was the son of Hardee King and the grandson of Roswell III and Mariah Guerard.

Miss West misled him into believing that she was a direct descendant of Roswell III. But the King family member from the north was just interested in finally meeting his long-forgotten African-American relatives.

In this small town of Riceboro, Georgia, where the population was about 745 people in the early 1990s and the racial makeup of African-Americans was more than 88 percent, everybody knew everybody. And having a white person she had never seen before asking questions about one of their residents, well, Miss West was being a little protective because she was afraid of what the visiting person's agenda would be. That was why Miss West had misled him.

After their brief meeting, he left his phone number with Miss West and they agreed to meet the next day at a local church parking lot. The next day, he did not show up. So later that day, Miss West told her sister Rosella about the visitor, saying, "A white person came here asking for the Black descendants of Roswell King III." Mrs. Rosella knew right away who he was looking for since her husband was one of the Black King's descendants. The next day, Mrs. Rosella made a phone call to her niece Geneva Jones, who was also related to Roswell III. Mrs. Rosella told her niece everything—that a person was looking for his Black family. During the phone conversation, She gave the contact phone number of the person to her niece, Geneva. Geneva is the daughter of Annie (King) Wilkins, and the great-granddaughter of Roswell King III and Mariah Guerard.

A couple of days passed, and a member of the Black King family finally contacted the man and arranged a meeting between the two families. The King family of northern Georgia and the Black King family of coastal Georgia finally met in February 2001.

Newspaper articles were published in the *Atlanta Journal-Constitution* (*AJC*) in February 2001 titled, "Distant family past obscures more recent era" and "My family tree." The articles were about the King family from north Georgia uniting with their distant cousins from coastal Georgia.

Later that day, the two families visited the location of Roswell King's South Hampton Island and Darien, Georgia, a town in McIntosh County. In the Article, a photograph was taken of the two families under the big oak tree in South Hampton Island; it was the same oak tree the King's grandchildren played under in 1924 when men came to their home and ran Mariah Guerard and her family off the land. The second photograph was taken of the two families standing next to the graves in Darien where some of the King's relatives were buried.

In the 1990s Miss Lois Simpson met an inspiring woman named Sarah Lee Winner. Sarah befriended the eighty-two-year-old Lois and moved into Barrington Hall by gaining her trust in friendship. Miss Lois was listed as the caretaker of Barrington Hall. At some point, Miss Lois's relationship with Barrington Hall changed from being the caretaker to the trustee. Sarah created a living trust to make Miss Lois the trustee of Barrington Hall. On February 4, 2002, Miss Lois, at an old age, appointed Sarah as trustee of the Lois Virginia King Simpson Trust, under a deed of gift filed on record. Sarah's intentions may have been somewhat self-interested; she and her family had invested in real estate—commercial and residential—for several years in the past.

The question now is, how did Lois Virginia King Simpson become the trustee of the estate and property when the original trust of the estate and property were conveyed to Roswell King III by Barrington King? In the Fulton County deed indices, there are more than eighty entries where Sarah

The Inheritance

is listed as a party to the transactions. On one occasion, it appears that several of her real estate transactions appeared to be improper flips, somehow granting her as the trustee of Barrington Hall. Additionally, although she held the title to the property as a trustee, she had encumbered a portion of the Barrington Hall property, which was previously unencumbered with debt, which was a $400,000-dollar high-interest mortgage, listed in Fulton County Deed Book 34459, page 563.[29] This was also discovered during a certificate of title search and public records search in Fulton County, Georgia.

According to Sarah, the loan proceeds were used to make improvements to Barrington Hall. Interestingly, she executed the mortgage as an individual rather than as the trustee of the trust. And after the loan closed, there were several canceled mortgages on other mortgages where she as an individual was the debtor. But in the end, the new owner did a beautiful job with the restoration of Barrington Hall with the money that was loaned.

Lois Virginia King Simpson died on May 26, 2003 leaving the estate of Barrington Hall completely in the hands of Sarah. Several of the King relatives attended Miss Lois's funeral in Roswell, Georgia. Her body was not buried; it was cremated and placed in an urn. Until this date, Miss Lois's urn has been missing from the cemetery. Miss Lois's questionable death had the King family members wondering who had the urn of Miss Lois King Simpson's remains. Why was it moved from the cemetery, and by whom? Was it a family member of Miss Lois, or was someone trying to cover up something?

In June 2003 a witness saw and read the will that was written by Roswell King III at the home of the historical Barrington Hall. The whereabouts of the will was kept secret for decades and was never put into probate. The will was found in a closet at Barrington Hall shortly after the passing of Miss Lois.

Did Miss Katherine and Miss Lois know the will was located at Barrington Hall? Or did any of the previous caretakers and residents know of the will? If so, they would be at high risk of losing the estate.

After learning of a will's existence from Roswell III, the Black King family called a meeting with the other local family members to try to obtain a copy of the decades-old will from their great-grandfather.

Since Roswell III's will was never offered for probate, they could not get a copy of his will from the courthouse. The will mentioned that Roswell King's second family from coastal Georgia was entitled to a trust fund. The Black family consisted of Roswell King III and Mariah Guerard's children. Now, the descendant from the family decided to hire a lawyer to find out what was in the trust fund. The trust was considered to be a living trust that was originally established for Roswell King III.

In August 2003 the family decided to find the best lawyer for our case. They searched the internet, and they also researched information about lawyers in the Library of Congress. They checked the credentials of many lawyers and law firms and found one listed among the top law firms in the country. The family hired the law office to perform a certificate of title search and public records search in Fulton County, Georgia, hoping to find any information about Roswell King III's will, the trust, and Barrington Hall.

In the report and findings about Barrington Hall, it was mentioned in the deed book in Fulton County that there were missing pages from the estate records. Next, we wanted the law firm to look into the trust fund of Roswell III. The lawyer stated that there was a trust fund worth a substantial sum of money in a vault and it belonged to someone, but without Roswell III's will, the law firm could not prove to whom it belonged. After a few weeks of working on our case, the lawyer called the family and said that he was backing out of the case and that he could not go on any further. And he would return the remainder of the retainer.

Mysteriously, the case was dropped by the law firm. The family asked, "Why are you backing out now?" The lawyer further stated, "I cannot get into specific details, but you need to leave it alone." We believe he was pressured by someone higher up to drop our case. It was said by a paralegal, "This thing is bigger than the mob." Meaning the deeds to Barrington Hall's estate, the living trust, and any other matters about the King family's legal documents were tied up in many distributions of wealth. Because of this and without the will, the King family in coastal Georgia did not go any further with the case, since they did not have evidence that Roswell III conveyed his inheritance to his second family.

In April 2004 two articles were written in the *Atlanta Journal-Constitution*. One of the articles conveyed, *the fate of the landmark home was questionable when the last of the King heirs died in 2000*. I assume this article was referring to the death of the eighty-three-year-old Lois Virginia King Simpson in May 2003. Remember, Miss Lois was not a blood relative to the Kings, so she could not possibly be the last of the King heirs.

The other article conveyed, through a series of beneficial trusts, the house, which is Barrington Hall, and its contents were passed on to Sarah. Also, this article stated the same as the previous article: Miss Lois was referred to as the last of the King heirs. These articles were inaccurate, and they upset and offended the entire King family, including the King family of northern and coastal Georgia.

In response, the newspaper apologized that it had upset in the King family with the articles. The articles intended to focus on the house and its restoration. As a longtime resident of Atlanta and the Roswell area, the editor claimed she was aware of the story of Miss Katherine and Miss Lois. The term "last of the King heirs" was an editorial "fix" that the editor thought clarified who inherited the house. The newspaper knew other King descendants survived and had met some of them at meetings and other events. The newspaper online today does not show the original articles, but the family has the original paper clippings of the newspaper articles from 2004.

In 2005, after the lovely restoration of Barrington Hall, Sarah sold the Barrington Hall subdivision to Holton and Associates. Since then, Sarah's name has been expunged from the online articles, but newspaper clippings have been obtained. During the time the house was sold, members of the King family went to the house to retrieve some important artifacts and documents. Supposedly, a copy of Roswell King III's will was among the documents. Later in 2005, the city of Roswell purchased Barrington Hall. Now the home is back within the King's lineage.

This is a declaration about human equality. Historically, the Black descendants of Roswell King III have not been treated with these rights. Hopefully, justice can resolve the inequalities that haunted Roswell III's second family in coastal Georgia for more than a century.

I am the third generation of Hardee King, who is the oldest son of Roswell King III and Mariah Guerard, the fourth generation of Roswell King Jr., and the fifth generation of Roswell King Sr. We are the heirs to Roswell King's inheritance. In fact, there are many of Roswell III's Black descendants still alive today and living in coastal Georgia and Florida who are seeking answers about the unclaimed inheritance from our great-grandfather and great-great-grandfather, who is Roswell King III, and the land at South Hampton Island. We are truly the last of the King heirs who never received their inheritance.

"In any moment of decision, the best thing you can do is the right thing, the next-best thing is the wrong thing, and the worst thing you can do is nothing." —Theodore Roosevelt.

A Prayer for the King Family:

Heavenly Father the most high, I am not coming to you in my own name, but by the Lord of host, the God of Israel. You are Lord of Lords, God of Gods, and King of Kings. The throne of Your glory is forever. Forever and ever is Your name sanctified and glorified. You are blessed and glorified. Father, You possess power over all things. You see all things, and nothing can be hidden from You. You are the creator. You are holy. And You are God almighty. Father, because of Your divine grace and Your love for me, You are worthy to be praised. And I will worship you, Father, in spirit and truth.

Father, I know You are faithful to do all that You say You are going to do. So Father, I want to thank You for all You have done for me. And I thank You for the things that You are about to do. Lord, I pray to You in the time of Your favor; in Your great love, answer my prayers, O God, with Your sure salvation. Father, I pray to You for comfort, wisdom in Your words, healing, protection, prosperity, and Your blessings. I claim these blessings upon my life, and upon my family life.

Jesus, You said in Your words that whatever I ask for in prayer, believe that I have received it, and it will be done. Lord, today I pray for increase. I pray to You in faith, and without a doubt in my mind. I am receiving all that is due to me. The enemy has come to steal, kill, and destroy everything that belongs to me. I am reclaiming everything he has stolen from me, and wealth and riches are in my house.

Lord Jesus Christ, I believe that You are the son of God and the only way to God. And that You have died on the cross for my sins, and risen again from the dead. I accept You, Jesus, as my Lord and Savior! I surrender myself to You, Lord. And I will pick up my cross and follow You. Jesus, on the cross You have made a sacrifice, that I might be redeemed from the iniquity of my sins, from my transgression, any curses against my life.

Father, I know I do not only wrestle against flesh and blood but against principalities, against the rulers of the darkness, and against spiritual hosts of wickedness. Isaiah 54:17 states, "No weapon formed against You shall prosper, and every tongue which rises against me in judgment You shall condemn. This is the heritage of the servants of the Lord, and their righteousness is from me," says the Lord. Therefore, what the enemy uses to hurt me, God uses to prosper me. For I am redeemed from my sins. I am redeemed from the curses of the law. I am redeemed from poverty. I am redeemed from sickness. I am redeemed from financial debt. I am redeemed from spiritual death. I overcome it all, because greater than he that is in me than he that is within the world.

Lord, I ask for Your forgiveness. Father, forgive me for my sins, as I forgive others that have sinned against me. I forgive any person who ever harmed me or wronged me. I have forgiven them as God has forgiven me. Lord, I confess any sins committed by me, or by my ancestors. And now Lord, having received by faith Your forgiveness, with the authority I have by the child of God, I now release myself and those under my authority for any sins and any curses over my life. Jesus, You said whatsoever is bound on earth will be bound in heaven, and whatever is loose on earth will be loosed in heaven.

For the God that is in me, I know I can do all things through Christ who strengthens me. You are Elohim, the source of my strength. You are the one and only true God. You are my Jehovah Nissi, my banner that reminds me that You have already won the victory. You are my Jehovah Jireh, my provider in times of need. You are my Jehovah Rapha, my healer in both body and soul. You are my Jehovah Rohi, my Shepherd who watches over me.

Continue to watch over me Lord. Keep Your guardian angels around me and protect me daily. Protect my family, protect my home, protect my land, protect my health, protect my finances. Grant me extraordinary favors. Guide me in the path of righteousness. Guide me to do Your will.

A Prayer for the King Family:

Father, I am certain I have complete trust, and I am confident that I have received the blessings I asked for in this prayer. I have received them. And they will be done. God, thank You for hearing my prayers. For I know that You hear my prayers always. In Jesus's name, I pray to You. Amen.

The Genealogy of Roswell King III's Second Family:

These are the descendants of Roswell King III (1836–1911) and Mariah Guerard (1861–1938), who are the last of the King heirs.

1. Hardee King (1884–1944) married Rosa Quarterman and had eight (8) children.

    (1). Peter King (1897–1959), married Pearl F. (1892–1967). Peter had no children.
    (2). Jessie King (1907–1981), never married Frances. Jessie had one child from another woman.
    (3). Annie King (1911–1990), married Josh Wilkins Sr. and had four children.
    (4). Ernest King, married Nancy West. Ernest had one child; and later married Rosella West.
    (5). Everlena King, married Randolph Roberts and had two children.
    (6). Henry King died at the age of 9 years old
    (7). Robert King, married Rita and had no children.
    (8). Lula King, never married, but had one child.

2. Eddie King (1894–1943), never married and had no children.
3. Rosa King never married, but had three children.

- (1). Frances (Babe) King (1906–2000), first married George Curtis; and married to Willie Caple. She had no children.
- (2). Johnny King died by drowning in the Hampton River. He had no children.
- (3). Mamie King, married Ismond Jones. She had no children.

4. Eva King (1894–1978), married Robert Cook. They had one child. Later married Lawrence Jones. They had no children.

- (1). Roswell "Ross" Cook.

5. Mariah King, married Edward Cook. She had no children.
6. Marie King died at sixteen. She was never married and had no children.

Sources:

1. Robert M. Myers, *The Children of Pride: A True Story of Georgia and the Civil War* (New Haven: Yale University Press, 1972, 1585).

2. Ibid.

3. Ibid.

4. Charles Colcock Jones, *The Religious Instruction of the Negroes in the United States* (Savannah: Thomas Purse, 1842,52,58,64,81).

5. Myers, *The Children of Pride*, 1585.

6. Ibid.

7. Ibid.

8. Ibid.

9. Ibid.

10. Lawyer Offices Cheney & Cheney, P.C., "2006 Certificate of Title Search," Public Records of Liberty County, Georgia, Law Firm in Reidsville, Georgia (Wilkins-King family's copy).

11. Myers, *The Children of Pride*.

12. U.S. Census Bureau, "1910 U.S. Population Census of Georgia (Microfilm)," Georgia Historical Society, Savannah.

13. The editors of Americans All *(c.1877 - c.1967)*, "**Jim Crow Laws: Florida and Georgia** - Code, Colored, Constitution, Descendant, Felony, Intermarriage, Legislature, Mulatto, Negro, Nurse, Ordinance, Penal Code, Public Transportation, Railroads, Schools, Segregation, Separate

But Equal, Slavery, Statute, Supreme Court, Voting, Waiting Rooms,"The People of America Foundation, retrieved May 31, 2023, https://americansall.org/legacy-story-group/jim-crow-laws-florida-and-georgia.

14. Myers, *The Children of Pride*.

15. Nadra K. Nittle, "The Short-Lived Promise of '40 Acres and a Mule,'" A&E Television Networks, posted November 9, 2022, retrieved May 31, 2023, https://www.history.com/news/40-acres-mule-promise.

16. U.S. Census Bureau, "1910 U.S. Census Population of Georgia."

17. Cheney & Cheney, "2006 Certificate of Title Search."

18. Ibid.

19. Ibid.

20. Ibid.

21. Ibid.

22. Ibid.

23. Ibid.

24. Kaufman, Chaiken, Miller, & Klorfein: Attorneys and Counselors at Law, "2003 Certificate of Title Search," Public Records of Fulton County, Georgia (Wilkins-King family's copy).

25. Ibid.

26. Ibid.

27. Cheney & Cheney, "2006 Certificate of Title Search."

28. Kaufman, Chaiken, Miller, & Klorfein, "2003 Certificate of Title Search."

29. Cheney & Cheney, "2006 Certificate of Title Search."

Photograph Credits:

Insert 1
Roswell King III portrait. By inheritance of Eva (King) Jones. (Wilkins-King Family Archives)

Insert 2
Mariah Guerard portrait. By inheritance of Eva (King) Jones. (Wilkins-King Family Archives)

Insert 3
Map of Coastal Georgia drawing. By Danny Jones. (Map drawing)

Insert 4
Annie (King) Wikins photograph. By inheritance of Geneva (Wilkins) Jones. (Wilkins-King Family Archives)

Insert 5
Robert King, and Frances (King) Caple setting together. By inheritance Geneva Wilkins-Jones. (Wilkins-King Family Archives)

Insert 6
Lula King standing with two friends. By inheritance of Geneva (Wilkins) Jones. (Wilkins-King Family Archives)

Insert 7
Rosa King portrait. By inheritance of Geneva (Wilkins) Jones. (Wilkins-King Family Archives)

Insert 8
Eva (King) Jones setting on coach. By inheritance of Eva (King) Jones. (Wilkins-King Family Archives)

Insert 9
Eva (King) Jones setting on coach holding hand fan. By inheritance of Eva (King) Jones. (Wilkins-King Family Archives)

Insert 10
Marie King portrait. By inheritance of Eva (King) Jones. (Wilkins-King Family Archives)

Insert 11
Marie King portrait of a side view. By inheritance of Eva (King) Jones. (Wilkins-King Family Archives)

Insert 12
Frances (King) Caples self-photograph. By inheritance of Geneva (Wilkins) Jones. (Wilkins-King Family Archives)

Insert 13
Frances (King) Caples photograph of Hair show. By inheritance of Geneva (Wilkins) Jones. (Wilkins-King Family Archives)

Insert 14
Frances (King) Caples photograph of her league cricket sport team in 1930s. By inheritance of Geneva (Wilkins) Jones. (Wilkins-King Family Archives)

Photograph Credits:

Insert 15
Johnny King portrait. By inheritance of Eva (King) Jones. (Wilkins-King Family Archives)

Insert 16
Roswell Cook and Estella Roberts photograph. By inheritance of Eva (King) Jones. (Wilkins-King Family Archives)

Insert 17
Roswell Cook and Eve (King) Cook-Jones photograph. By inheritance of Eva (King) Jones. (Wilkins-King Family Archives).

Printed in the USA
CPSIA information can be obtained
at www.ICGtesting.com
CBHW051652140824
13126CB00056B/1416

9 781662 896408